Bible Fun Stuff

FOR AGES 11-

Design
and Devour

David C Cook

transforming lives together

DESIGN AND DEVOUR
Published by David C. Cook
4050 Lee Vance View
Colorado Springs, CO 80918 U.S.A.

David C. Cook Distribution Canada
55 Woodslee Avenue, Paris, Ontario, Canada N3L 3E5

David C. Cook U.K., Kingsway Communications
Eastbourne, East Sussex BN23 6NT, England

David C. Cook and the graphic circle C logo
are registered trademarks of Cook Communications Ministries.

Written by Frieda Nossaman
Cover Design by BMB Design/Scott Johnson
Interior Design by TrueBlue Design/Sandy Flewelling
Photography © Brad Armstrong Photography
Illustrations by Kris & Sharon Cartwright, Joan Loitz, Josep Anton Mas Elvira, Kathy Konkle

Scripture quotations, unless otherwise noted, are from
the HOLY BIBLE, NEW INTERNATIONAL VERSION.
Copyright © 1973, 1978, 1984 by International Bible Society.
Used by permission of Zondervan Publishing House. All rights reserved.

ISBN 978-1-4347-6721-9

First Printing 2009
Printed in the United States

1 2 3 4 5 6 7 8 9 10

transforming lives together

TABLE OF CONTENTS

HOW TO USE THIS BOOK

Whet your students' appetites for fun and food and turn your Sunday school room into a savory space! Open your kitchen cupboards and get ready to mix, stir, roll, and pour by bringing the Word to life as students learn to taste and see God is good! From spicy to sweet, students will cook up some wonderful snacks to share, give away, and devour that will make your Bible lessons unforgettable and delicious.

This book contains 26 simple recipes that will help middle school students connect with the Bible lesson in a new way. Students ages 11 to 14 like individuality, so many recipes have a "build your own" concept. Middle school students often struggle in positive interaction with one another, but cooking and creating together may cause their inhibitions to vanish as they create and enjoy their edible creations.

The 26 activities in this book can be done in any order and easily fit into any curriculum. Simply use the Scripture and Topic Index on page 110 to match a project with the lesson you're teaching. These activities also can be used as alternate Step Three activities in several curriculum lines: David C. Cook Bible-In-Life, Echoes, LifeLINKS to God, College Press, Reformation Press, Wesley, Anglican, and The Cross. If you have one of these lines, look through the Correlation Chart on page 111 and find the activity geared to your lesson. You'll use this new activity instead of one of the other Step Three activities listed in your teacher's guide. This book, when combined with *How's Your Serve?*, will give you a full year's worth of Step Three replacement activities for the middle-school age group.

HELPFUL HINTS

Here are some things to keep in mind:

- Food allergies are on the rise. Although many food allergies are outgrown by the time a student reaches middle school, some are not. The lessons have alternative ingredients for the most common allergies—milk, wheat, and peanuts. However, we have included an allergy alert letter so parents can inform you of any allergies students may have. (Please see page 112.)
- Clean hands count! Students ideally should wash their hands for at least 30 seconds with soap and water. Keep a ready supply of hand wipes available as an alternative. Also remind students to avoid touching their face or hair while preparing food.
- Prior to creating these edible projects, check the ingredients list and factor in how many students you typically have in your group. Note which ingredients are used more than once and buy those items in bulk if possible. If cost is an issue, ask volunteers to bring one item or have students bring ingredients on a rotating cycle (just be sure to remind them and their parent or guardian). Always err on the side of more food rather than too little.
- Some food items will need to be kept in a cooler or refrigerator until ready to use. Also, some recipes may call for specific tools, such as a slow cooker. Double-checking all items will save you from having to make a trip back home or having to borrow a necessity at the last minute. If you have ingredients on hand that would work in the recipes, feel free to incorporate them—be creative!
- These edible projects have been planned with middle school students' tastes in mind, but consider personal preferences. Don't force anyone to eat anything they don't want to. You'll be sending each recipe home so there's always another chance for the students to try something at a later time.
- Make cleanup a snap by individually wrapping each ingredient and using waxed paper or foil under projects as applicable. Keep clean rags, a mop, paper towels, and plenty of napkins handy.

So, open your cupboards and turn the page. You and your students are in for some delicious fun!

UNIQUELY CREATED!

ROLL-UP CREATIONS THAT ARE OUT OF THIS WORLD!

BIBLE BASIS:
Genesis 1:1–26

MEMORY VERSE:
But God made the earth by his power; he founded the world by his wisdom and stretched out the heavens by his understanding.
Jeremiah 10:12

BIBLE BACKGROUND

Creation. It's one of the most astounding events recorded in the Bible, yet too often we gloss over how incredible the moment of Creation really was. Imagine—God made everything out of nothing by the power of His word.

Genesis 1:1 says, "In the beginning God created the heavens and the earth." By middle school, many students have had their belief in Creation questioned: "How can you believe the earth was created in seven days?" "Isn't evolution more scientific than Creation?" "Creation can't be proven . . . and all scientific theories need to be proven, don't they?" These comments seemingly bombard students who believe Genesis offers the true explanation for the earth's existence.

Remind students that our awesome God created all they see—sky, sea, birds, fish, animals, and everything else, including humans who are a made in God's image. Jeremiah 10:12 says, "But God made the earth by his power; he founded the world by his wisdom and stretched out the heavens by his understanding." Christians aren't called to fight with those who take offense at this truth; rather, we are to lovingly proclaim the truth about the awesome God who made everything. When we do, the Holy Spirit steps in at the right time to reveal the truth to those ready to receive it.

So, take a look around. Breathe in the fresh air, listen for a bird's song, gaze out at the blue sky, and praise the awesome One who made it all . . . out of nothing.

HINTS FROM THE KITCHEN

- These sliced roll-ups look like starry galaxies, little reminders of God's creation.

- An easy way to manage a larger group of students for this activity is to arrange the ingredients and supplies in a two-sided assembly line on a table. For large groups, provide more than one line. Students move down both sides of the assembly line after you explain or demonstrate the complete process. Ask those who finish to wait to eat until all have been through the line.

- Dice the tomatoes and the optional jalapeño peppers ahead of time. (You might want to wear disposable gloves to dice the peppers.) Then put the tomatoes and peppers into separate bowls.

- Keep packages of turkey or ham sealed up until students are ready to begin making their roll-ups. At that time, open the package and spread the slices on plates.

- If cream cheese is in a plastic tub, leave it as it is. If it's a block wrapped in foil, remove the cheese and put it on a plate.

- Tortillas stay fresher if you keep them in the package until just before use. When students are ready, either dole them out one at a time or spread the tortillas on a plate so the students can easily grab what they need.

INGREDIENTS & SUPPLIES (SERVES 10)

- ❑ 1 pkg. large tortillas (1 tortilla per student)
- ❑ 1–2 pkgs. thin-sliced sandwich turkey or ham (1 or 2 slices per student)
- ❑ One 8 oz. pkg. cream cheese (about 2 tablespoons per student)
- ❑ Two 14.5 oz. cans diced tomatoes or 2 ½ cups diced fresh tomatoes
- ❑ Paper or plastic bowls
- ❑ Plastic or disposable plates
- ❑ Serving utensils
- ❑ Plastic spoons and serrated knives
- ❑ Toothpicks
- ❑ Optional: Two 4 oz. cans diced jalapeños

CREATIVE COOKERY

ALLERGY WARNING: *If you have a chef with dairy allergies, the cream cheese could be a problem. Mustard or another condiment may be substituted. Also, the jalapeños should be left out for students sensitive to spicy foods. For kids with wheat allergies, corn tortillas may be an alternative (but be sure to ask).*

The most important rule of making a roll-up is to not overstuff it. Having ample ingredients is important but roll-ups will fall apart when cut if too many things are on top of each other.

1. Dice tomatoes and jalapeños beforehand, if necessary.

2. Show the students how to spread cream cheese on their tortillas, how to place meats on top of the cream cheese, and then how to add tomatoes and jalapeños.

3. Demonstrate rolling the tortilla. (Be gentle so the ingredients don't spill out.) Roll until the covered tortilla is completely rolled up.

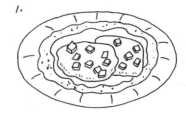

4. Using a plastic serrated knife, carefully slice the tortilla roll-up into 1-inch or ½-inch thick slices (depending on preference). Cut two or three pieces at a time before separating the roll-ups from the tortilla. Place roll-up slices on a plate and secure each with a toothpick.

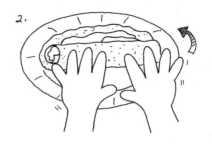

5. When all students have finished their preparations, say a prayer asking God to bless the food or call on a student to do so. Finally, carefully pick up and enjoy your roll-ups, removing the toothpick just before eating each roll-up.

SAVOR IT!

We have a small taste of God's creative power in our own lives. As we are made in God's image, God the Creator has made us capable of creating with the things He has made and provided. It's an exciting and powerful gift. However, we may never fully understand many aspects of God's Creation, a reality which brings wonder and mystery to life. Some questions we can answer, however, are:

- **What things in God's creation show His awesome power and might?** *(Everything God created, including mountains; whales; the sun, moon and stars; etc.)*

- **What things show His awesome gentleness and beauty?** *(rainbows, butterflies, etc.)*

- **What made Adam and Eve different from all other things God created?** *(God made them in His image. He wanted a special relationship with them.)*

TORTILLA ROLL-UPS

Make as many of these as you please. Remember: The most important rule of making a roll-up is to not overstuff it. Having ample ingredients is important, but the roll-ups will fall apart if too many things are on top of each other.

RECIPE TO TAKE HOME

Ingredients:
- ❑ 1 large tortilla
- ❑ 1 or 2 slices of turkey or ham
- ❑ 2 tablespoons cream cheese
- ❑ Diced tomato (¼ cup)
- ❑ Optional: diced jalapeños

Supplies:
- ❑ Plate or paper plate
- ❑ Dull knife for spreading ingredients
- ❑ Serrated plastic knife (or, with adult approval, use a metal serrated knife) to cut roll-ups apart
- ❑ Toothpicks

Directions:
1. Cut a ripe tomato into small pieces or open up a can of diced tomatoes. Put tomatoes into a small bowl.
2. Take a large tortilla and put it on a plate. Spread cream cheese on one side of the tortilla. Place thin slices of ham or turkey on the cheese and then add the tomatoes. If you dare, sprinkle on a few jalapeños.
3. Use your fingers to roll the tortilla.
4. With a serrated plastic knife (or, with adult supervision, a metal serrated knife) cut the roll-up into ½-inch to 1-inch slices. Carefully place the roll-up slices on a plate and stick a toothpick through the middle to keep the rolls from falling apart. Enjoy (just be sure to remove the toothpicks before eating)!

FOLLOWING GOD'S TRAIL

PICK YOUR FAVORITE TRAIL MIX SURPRISES.

BIBLE BASIS:
Genesis 1:28–31;
2:8–9, 15–17

MEMORY VERSE:
The earth is the LORD's,
and everything in it,
the world, and all
who live in it.
Psalm 24:1

BIBLE BACKGROUND

Have you ever wondered why God created you? Not just people in general, but the one and only you? Genesis 1 and 2 shed light on our existence and offer renewed purpose for living. God created all humans with specific jobs to do. Sure, He could have created more people in the same way as He created Adam and Eve, but He didn't choose that route. Instead, God instructed Adam and Eve to "be fruitful and increase in number; fill the earth and subdue it " (Gen. 1:28). A pretty daunting task if you consider that they were to become the original parents of everyone on earth. In C. S. Lewis' novel *The Lion, The Witch, and the Wardrobe* the children who enter Narnia are called sons of Adam and daughters of Eve. Technically, that's just what we all are.

God's commands to Adam and Eve still apply today. We still share the purpose they were given. Each of us also has individual purposes given to us by God that He will fulfill as we faithfully follow Him (Ps. 57:2; 1 Cor. 12). Additionally, the Bible brims over with verses affirming how special you are to God (Matt. 10:29–31; Eph. 5:1–2; Ps. 100:3; 1 John 4:19; Eph. 3:17–19). Find your purpose today through God's eyes. You'll never regret following God's plan, a trail blazed especially for you.

HINTS FROM THE KITCHEN

- ▐●▌ Teach your students that God made them for a purpose. At the same time, remind them that they were created unique and with different talents. Today's edible project allows students to blaze their own trail as they make personalized blends of trail mix.

- ▐●▌ To simplify assembly, set up small round tables with ingredients and supplies spread out across the area or a long table with enough room for students to move easily about and reach items.

- ▐●▌ Do not include any nut products or items manufactured in nut facilities if there are people with nut allergies in your group. Also, some banana chips are fried in peanut oil, so check your ingredients if allergies are a concern.

- ▐●▌ If you have budget restraints, stick with inexpensive fillers: air-popped popcorn, raisins, chocolate or carob chips, puffed rice, cereal pieces, or pretzels. Other items you may want to consider are: candy-coated chocolate pieces, cranberries, dried apricots, white-chocolate chips, yogurt-covered raisins or pretzels, and banana chips.

- ▐●▌ Provide a sturdy, resealable plastic bag for each student and have students write their names on their bags. If there is an abundance of snacks, you may want to provide two or three bags: one for sweet items, one for salty items, and another to mix things up.

Encourage students to place at least three types of items in their bags so they'll have a true mix.

INGREDIENTS & SUPPLIES

- ❑ Various trail mix ingredients such as air-popped popcorn, raisins, chocolate or carob chips, puffed rice, cereal pieces or pretzels, candy-coated chocolate pieces, cranberries, dried apricots, white-chocolate chips, yogurt-covered raisins or pretzels, and banana chips. (Plan on ½ cup of the larger ingredients and ¼ cup of the smaller ingredients per student.)
- ❑ Serving bowls and spoons (one per ingredient used)
- ❑ Permanent marker
- ❑ Sturdy, resealable, sandwich-sized plastic bags (at least 1 per student)

CREATIVE COOKERY

__ALLERGY WARNING:__ Do not include any nuts or items that were packaged in a facility that processes nuts. Some banana chips are fried in peanut oil, so check the packaging.

Allow students to mix and match their favorite ingredients. All sweet, all salty, and a mix of the two all make for great snacking.

1. Give each student at least one sturdy, resealable plastic bag and instruct him or her to write his or her name on it with the permanent marker.

2. Allow students to visit the tables with the ingredient-filled bowls and add whatever items they like in their plastic bag.

3. Instruct students to squeeze most of the air out of their bags when they are filled about halfway. Then have them seal their bags and gently shake them to mix things up.

4. Allow students to eat their creations or take them home with them.

shake bag

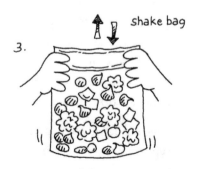

SAVOR IT!

We might meet many people whose only purpose is to live for themselves. They may seem successful or popular now, but that doesn't last. Only what is done for God's kingdom will last for eternity. If your purpose is in line with God's, you will find true success in His eyes.

But following God's trail, or purpose for you, means staying in His will, seeking out what the Bible says, and praying about every important decision. It isn't always easy to know God's purpose, but if you seek to find out, God will reward you by directing your life.

- **What purpose did God give to the first people He created?** *(to have children, to care for the earth, etc.)*

- **How might God show us His purposes for us?** *(through the Bible, through prayer, through His people, through circumstances, etc.)*

- **What are some ways you have experienced God's direction in your life?** *(Answers will vary.)*

GOD'S TRAIL MIX

Remember—you can't have too many fun ingredients in trail mix. Use some things from your pantry at home to see if they add extra chewiness or crunch.

Ingredients:
- ❑ Air-popped popcorn, raisins, chocolate or carob chips, puffed rice, cereal pieces or pretzels, candy-coated chocolate pieces, cranberries, dried apricots, white-chocolate chips, yogurt-covered raisins or pretzels, and banana chips. *(Note: some banana chips are fried in peanut oil. Check your ingredients if allergies are a concern.)*

Supplies:
- ❑ Sturdy, resealable quart-sized plastic bag(s), 1 or more

Directions:
1. Open your resealable plastic bag and fill with your favorite trail mix ingredients. Remember you can make it all sweet, all salty, or a little bit of both.
2. Take it with you to eat after a long hike or sports workout. These mixes make great gifts too. Put the mix in a pretty serving dish or container, add a ribbon, and you're set. Tape an ingredients list on the bottom in case your friend has any allergies.

SAVED FROM OUR DIRT

GOD CAN MAKE A FLOWER OUT OF OUR "DIRT."

BIBLE BASIS:
Genesis 3:1–19;
Romans 5:12, 19

MEMORY VERSE:
For just as through the disobedience of the one man the many were made sinners, so also through the obedience of the one man the many will be made righteous. *Romans 5:19*

BIBLE BACKGROUND

We all sin, even Christians. Romans 3:23 says, "For all have sinned and fall short of the glory of God." We don't generally like to think of ourselves as sinners, do we? We'd rather people see only the good things we do . . . but good works won't get us to heaven. The only way to get there is by trusting in the salvation God provides through His Son Jesus Christ. We're called to good living but we need first to place our faith in Jesus in order to truly live for God. If we think we have no sin, then we essentially are saying we don't need Jesus. That isn't what God wants at all. First John 1:8–10 says, "If we claim to be without sin, we deceive ourselves and the truth is not in us. If we confess our sins, he is faithful and just and will forgive us our sins and purify us from all unrighteousness. If we claim we have not sinned, we make him out to be a liar and his word has no place in our lives." Pretty strong words!

In Genesis 3:1–19 we see how Adam and Eve fell into sin's trap when they listened to Satan. God told them not to eat of the tree from the middle of the garden or they would die (Gen. 2:17). Satan challenged God's instruction by saying, "You will not surely die . . . God knows that when you eat of it your eyes will be opened, and you will be like God, knowing good and evil" (Gen. 3:4–5). Eve ate the fruit and gave some to Adam. Then the eyes of both of them were opened and they realized they were naked. They hid from God for the first time when He came to walk with them in the garden. Sin separated them from God and it separates us from Him today. Jesus' death and resurrection is the only way we can be reconciled with God. As Romans 5:19 says, "For just as through the disobedience of the one man the many were made sinners, so also through the obedience of the one man the many will be made righteous."

HINTS FROM THE KITCHEN

- 🍽 Middle school students are aware of their sinfulness. With their growing maturity and responsibility comes independence and opportunities for more trouble, more often. As children grow up they hit periods where they test what they know. This isn't always bad, and can be positively directed; but it can lead to struggles and sins that can trap them. This tasty treat offers a sweet reminder that we can look to God for salvation from the dirt that sin causes in our lives.

- 🍽 Your students may have eaten a dessert like this before and may want to create it at home for a younger brother, sister, or friend.

- 🍽 Making the dirt is messy, so have students crush their cookies in a sealed plastic bag.

- 🍽 To minimize cleanup, cover the entire work area with a tarp or newsprint.

- 🍽 Disposable dishes make cleanup easier but using toy sand buckets and shovels (new ones) makes quite an impression. Be sure to wash containers thoroughly with soapy warm water and dry prior to use.

- 🍽 If the lollipop won't stand up on its own, lean it against the side of the dish or bucket.

- 🍽 Remind students that because Jesus conquered the dirty trap of sin, we can grow and flourish for Him.

INGREDIENTS & SUPPLIES (SERVES 10)

- ❏ Five 1 oz. boxes instant chocolate pudding or four 6-count pudding cup packages (2 cups per student)
- ❏ Milk (if using instant pudding. Follow instructions on pudding box for quantities)
- ❏ 1 package of chocolate sandwich cookies stuffed with white icing (about 5 cookies per student)
- ❏ Resealable plastic bag (1 per student)
- ❏ Disposable bowl and spoon, or new toy pail and shovel (1 per student)
- ❏ One 4.5 oz. bag candy worm gummies, either sweet or sour (at least 2 worms per student)
- ❏ 1 package colorful, plastic-wrapped lollipops
- ❏ Individual desks or long table where students can work
- ❏ Tarp or newsprint (enough to cover all work surfaces)

CREATIVE COOKERY

ALLERGY WARNING: The cookies may be an issue for students with wheat allergies. Ask if puffed rice cereal could serve as an alternative for some "crunch" in the dirt snack.

Playing in the "dirt" has never been so much fun.

1. Give each student a bowl and a spoon or a toy pail and shovel that you washed ahead of time. Have students fill the bowls or pails with the pudding.

2. Hand each student a resealable plastic bag containing five cookies. Instruct them to finely crush the cookies with their fists, then carefully dump the crumbs into the pudding.

3. Use a spoon to stir the pudding and crushed cookies together.

4. Give each student at least two candy worm gummies and have students stick them into or on top of the dirt.

5. Provide each student with a colorful lollipop wrapped in plastic. Have them stick their lollipop in the middle of the dirt to represent a flower.

6. Say a prayer or have a volunteer pray to thank God that He has forgiven us of our "dirt" and to bless the food.

7. Use a spoon or toy shovel to dig in and enjoy.

SAVOR IT!

We all sin and have need for a Savior. God provides salvation through Jesus. We won't be trapped by our sins if we confess them. Jesus has taken care of the rest. We can trust Him to forgive our confessed sins.

- **What kinds of sins do you see your peers getting caught up in?** (*students may say lying, cheating, stealing, being reckless or careless with others' property, fighting with siblings or parents, etc.*)

- **When you are caught up in these kinds of sins, how do you feel?** (*frustrated, mad, guilty, stressed, wanting to please others but unable to make everyone happy, etc.*)

- **How does knowing Jesus as your Savior give you hope when you sin?** (*Jesus is always ready to forgive no matter what the sin, He loves us even though we sin, we can ask for forgiveness, etc.*)

DIRT GARDEN

Give this recipe as a gift to a friend or make it for a family member. Younger kids, especially, will enjoy it.

Ingredients:
- ❑ 1 cup of chocolate pudding or 2 pudding cups
- ❑ 5 chocolate sandwich cookies stuffed with white icing
- ❑ Sweet or sour candy worm gummies
- ❑ Colorful lollipop

Supplies:
- ❑ Bowl and spoon or a toy pail and shovel (rinsed in soapy water beforehand)
- ❑ Resealable plastic bag

Directions:
1. Fill your bowl or clean toy pail with the pudding.
2. Place five chocolate sandwich cookies stuffed with white icing into a resealable plastic bag and finely crush the cookies.
3. Carefully dump the cookie crumbs into the bowl or pail of chocolate pudding.
4. Use a spoon or toy shovel to stir the pudding and crushed cookies together.
5. Add candy worm gummies and either stick them under the dirt or have them poke above the dirt.
6. Stick a colorful lollipop in the center of the dirt to represent a flower. If the lollipop won't stand up on its own, lean it against the edge of the bowl or pail.
7. Use a spoon or toy shovel to dig in and enjoy.

RAINBOW TWISTS

CELEBRATE GOD'S PROMISE WITH AN EDIBLE CANDY RAINBOW.

BIBLE BASIS:
Genesis 6:9–10;
7:1–5; 8:18–22

MEMORY VERSE:
We wait in hope for the
LORD; he is our help and
our shield. In him our
hearts rejoice, for we
trust in his holy name.
Psalm 33:20–21

BIBLE BACKGROUND

Middle school students are at an age where they can grasp the reality of how horrific the flood actually was. God only saved the animals, Noah, and his family. Everyone else perished. Students who understand God's loving nature may struggle with this. Although God is loving, God also is just, and He acted justly. The sins of the people of Noah's time were great. God responded with justice but also in faithfulness, as demonstrated through God's rescue of Noah and his family.

Noah showed his faith in God by constructing the ark exactly as God commanded. He likely was ridiculed, yet he stayed on course. Genesis 7:5 says, "And Noah did all that the LORD commanded him." God brought the animals to Noah by twos, but of the animals considered clean he took seven (Gen. 7:2). Noah also took seven of each kind of bird (Gen. 7:3). Some of these clean animals and birds later served as Noah's sacrifices to God (Gen. 8:20).

Genesis 7:16 states that after everyone entered the ark, the Lord shut the door, as if an example of how God faithfully seals all who will honor and obey Him in His love. God was faithful to His people by protecting Noah's family, even during the dark period of sin on the earth that Genesis 6:1–8 describes. God reminds us of that faithfulness to Noah—and of His promise never to flood the earth like that again—every time He places a rainbow in the sky (Gen. 9:12–16).

HINTS FROM THE KITCHEN

- The multi-colored licorice rainbow twists students will use can be found in most candy sections of grocery stores or drug stores. If you can't locate these colorful licorice rainbow packs, try ordering them online.

- The colors/flavors that generally come in the packages are: red/strawberry, orange/orange, yellow/lemonade, green/watermelon, blue/blue raspberry, violet/grape. (Although most scientists define a rainbow as having seven colors, indigo is not usually shown in rainbow art.)

- Write the colors of a rainbow in order from the top down on a chalkboard for students to view as they work: red, orange, yellow, green, blue, violet.

- Have students create their rainbows on individual desks or at a large table depending on your work area.

INGREDIENTS & SUPPLIES
(SERVES 10)

- ❏ 2 bags of rainbow licorice (1 of each licorice color per student)
- ❏ Wax paper or tin foil, cut or torn into 10" x 8" pieces
- ❏ Gallon-size, resealable plastic bags

CREATIVE COOKERY

*ALLERGY WARNING: *Some brands of licorice contain flour. Check the package if wheat allergies are a concern.*

A colorful rainbow that tastes good too? Students will enjoy the bright colors, sticky texture, and fun challenge this rainbow offers.

1. Have students create a licorice rainbow by placing pieces side-by-side in an arc shape on a piece of wax paper or tin foil. The licorice should be placed in the following color sequence from top to bottom: red, orange, yellow, green, blue, violet. Explain that colors in a rainbow always appear in this order. (The licorice flavors that correspond with these colors are: strawberry, orange, lemonade, watermelon, blue raspberry, and grape.)

2. Have students gently squeeze the colors together on the wax paper, then lift the colorful rainbow off of the wax paper or tin foil and eat it all together. Or, they may peel one piece at a time to eat.

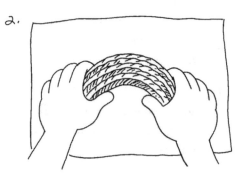

3. Offer gallon-size, resealable plastic bags for students to take home what they don't eat.

SAVOR IT!

Noah obeyed God even though God's commands probably were hard. Just the sheer size of the ark might have caused most people to throw in the towel. Noah, however, stuck with it, even though he was probably tired and possibly mocked. He knew he served a faithful God and he wanted to follow God's instructions exactly.

- **What do you think you would do if God assigned you a task like He gave to Noah?** (*Students might say they would obey, but press them to think about how they would feel if they actually had to make an ark or do something that people would obviously ridicule.*)

- **Why did God save Noah and his family?** (*Noah found favor with God and walked with God; Noah was obedient to God.*)

- **What did the rainbow represent to Noah?** (*God's promise to never send another flood that size.*)

RAINBOW TWISTS

This colorful rainbow will get the attention of everyone in your home. Sharing your rainbow or making extras would be a kind gesture!

Ingredients:
- ❑ 1 package rainbow licorice twists

Supplies:
- ❑ Wax paper or tin foil, cut or torn into a piece 10" wide by 8" tall
- ❑ 1 gallon-size, resealable plastic bag

Directions:
1. Create a rainbow from the licorice pieces by placing them onto the wax paper or tin foil.
2. Rainbow colors go in this order from the top going down: red, orange, yellow, green, blue, violet. (Although most scientists define a rainbow as having seven colors, indigo is not usually shown in rainbow art.) The licorice flavors that match these colors are: strawberry, orange, lemonade, watermelon, blue raspberry, and grape.
3. Lift your colorful rainbow off of the wax paper or tin foil and eat the pieces together or one piece at a time. Use a gallon-size, resealable plastic bag to save leftovers.

A BUEN APETITO APPETIZER

MINGLE WITH THIS FUN FIESTA PLATTER.

BIBLE BASIS:
Genesis 12:1–7

MEMORY VERSE:
I will instruct you and teach you in the way you should go; I will counsel you and watch over you. *Psalm 32:8*

BIBLE BACKGROUND

Obedience to God sometimes means taking on a challenging task, but it always places us exactly where God wants us to be.

God called Abram to move from Haran to the land of Canaan. Abram had already moved once before, from Ur to Haran. Instead of going all the way to Canaan as originally planned, Abram's family stopped and settled down. They didn't just live in Haran for a while . . . Abram's father lived to be 205 years old and Abram was already 75 when God told him to get moving! God promised Abram great things if he would "go to the land I will show you." God said, "I will make you into a great nation and I will bless you; I will make your name great, and you will be a blessing. I will bless those who bless you, and whoever curses you I will curse; and all peoples on earth will be blessed through you" (Gen. 12:2–3).

Abram might not have wanted to move at his age, but he didn't show it. Instead he did as the Lord told him and took his wife, Sarai, and his nephew Lot with him as well as all of their possessions. The Lord appeared to Abram and said, "To your offspring I will give this land." Abram built an altar there to the Lord, but he may have wondered how he and Sarai would have offspring, since they had no children and they were already beyond the age for having children. Abram continued on toward Canaan in obedience to the Lord. In time, God fulfilled all His promises to Abram, blessing him richly.

When we obey God, He can use even the most difficult circumstances for our ultimate benefit. Use this lesson to help your students see God's hand in their lives and His call for their obedience. Encourage your group by sharing about a time you obeyed God even though it was difficult, and tell what you learned through the experience.

HINTS FROM THE KITCHEN

- ◉ Often we serve appetizers at occasions to encourage mingling in large settings or at times we want people to feel comfortable in new crowds or places. Hovering over finger foods can help us feel relaxed or even somewhat in control of our situation. Similarly, we can feel at ease when we obey and remain in God's will. We're exactly where we need to be. Let today's appetizer snack serve as a reminder of this truth as your students mingle and become comfortable with one another while eating.

- ◉ Working together to make the layered dip in class will be almost as fun for your students as eating it.

- ◉ Keep in mind that some of these ingredients, such as sour cream and shredded cheese, need to be kept cold. Transport them in a cooler with ice cubes or ice packs. If a refrigerator is available, leave ingredients in it until just before making the snack.

- ◉ The snack isn't meant to be a meal; just make sure each student gets a chance to sample the items prepared. The key here is to enjoy tasting the food as a group.

INGREDIENTS & SUPPLIES (SERVES 10)

- ❑ Four 15 oz. cans bean dip
- ❑ Four 16 oz. containers sour cream
- ❑ Four 8 oz. packages shredded cheese (or 8 cups)
- ❑ 1 ripe tomato, diced, or one 14.5 oz can of diced tomatoes
- ❑ 1 small can of sliced or chopped black olives
- ❑ 2 bags pita bread (cut in slices) or tortilla chips
- ❑ Paper plates
- ❑ Spatulas or plastic spoons
- ❑ Can opener

CREATIVE COOKERY

ALLERGY WARNING: If you have a chef with dairy allergies, the cheese and sour cream could be a problem. For them, soy-based sour cream and cheese may be an alternative (or simply omit). If you have a student with wheat allergies, corn chips may serve as a great alternative to the pita bread or tortilla chips, but check with parents in advance.

This cold bean dip will disappear faster than you can get the chips out of the bag. Use this time to socialize, mingle, and enjoy hanging out.

1. Divide students into groups of three or four. The ingredients in the supply list will serve approximately ten to twelve students, or about three groups. Each group will receive a fourth of each ingredient in the supply list.

2. Use a can opener to open the bean dip. With a spatula or spoon, spread dip until the paper plate is covered.

3. Use a spatula or spoon to cover the bean dip with sour cream.

4. Layer shredded cheese on top.

5. Sprinkle with diced tomatoes.

6. Layer with black olives.

7. Serve with pita bread (cut into pieces) or tortilla chips.

8. Pray, thanking God for this opportunity to be together and for the food.

SAVOR IT!

Appetizers such as this bean dip are served at events where people mingle and chat with others they haven't met before or haven't seen for a while. Appetizers are not a meal but a snack that help people feel comfortable because it gives them something to do. We might say the appetizers help people have a feeling of control in a potentially uncomfortable situation.

God was in control when Abram was in the uncomfortable situation of moving. God is in control of your situation as well, no matter what's going on. When you obey God, you can be certain you're exactly where He wants you to be. He wants you to place your trust in Him and obey. You can know that He will be faithful.

- 🍽 **How do you think Abram might have felt about his move?** (*anxious, fearful, uncertain, questioning, confused, excited, hopeful, etc.*)

- 🍽 **Do you think Abram understood what God planned to do through Him? Why do you think that?** (*Answers will vary.*)

- 🍽 **Why is it sometimes hard to obey God?** (*we might feel pressure to do something else, we might not feel we have what it takes, etc.*)

- 🍽 **Why is it important to obey God?** (*Ultimately, because He is worthy of obedience, but also because He wants what is best for us and our growth in Him. It's the securest place to be, even if it isn't always easy.*)

TASTY BEAN DIP

Share this appetizer with a friend or serve it before a Mexican-style dinner. Everyone will be impressed. Be sure to have enough pita bread or tortilla chips on hand!

Ingredients:
- ❑ 15 oz. can of bean dip
- ❑ 16 oz. container of sour cream
- ❑ 8 oz. package of shredded cheese
- ❑ 1 ripe tomato, diced, or one 14.5 oz. can of diced tomatoes
- ❑ 6 oz. can sliced or chopped black olives
- ❑ Pita bread slices or tortilla chips

Supplies:
- ❑ Paper plate
- ❑ Can opener
- ❑ Spatula or plastic spoon

Directions:
1. Spread the bean dip on the plate with the spatula or spoon, covering most of the plate.
2. Use the spatula or spoon to cover the beans with sour cream.
3. Sprinkle cheese on top.
4. Add diced tomatoes on top of the cheese.
5. Layer the top with black olives.
6. Serve with pita bread or tortilla chips. ¡Buen Apetito!

STAINED-GLASS CROSSES

YOUR BELIEF IN GOD SHOWS THROUGH IN THIS COLORFUL DESIGN.

BIBLE BASIS:
Genesis 15:1–6;
Romans 4:1–5, 22–25

MEMORY VERSE:
For it is by grace you have been saved, through faith—and this not from yourselves, it is the gift of God.
Ephesians 2:8

BIBLE BACKGROUND

God promised Abram descendants as numerous as "the dust of the earth." Those words might have been difficult for Abram to understand since he didn't have a son. Yet Abram believed God. When Abram again approached God in faith, God reiterated His promise, this time saying that Abram's descendants would outnumber the stars. Abram trusted God's words even though he didn't know how they would come true. Genesis 15:6 confirms Abram believed the Lord and that God "credited it to him as righteousness." God was pleased with Abram's faith, and He revealed to Abram that a great nation would begin through his son.

In Romans 4:1–5, Paul used Abram's (God changed Abram's name to Abraham in Genesis 17) life to show how any person can be declared righteous by God if he puts his faith in Jesus Christ. Because of Christ's death and resurrection, those who have accepted Jesus into their hearts have assurance that they're righteous before God. Salvation can't be earned. It's a gift from God that must be accepted, nothing more. God's grace and love are the reason believers have assurance of salvation. God does change and mold the Christian in a process called sanctification. This process brings growth and maturity into the Christian's life but it can't save him or her in and of itself. As Romans 4:22–24 says of Abram, "This is why 'it was credited to him as righteousness.' The words 'it was credited to him' were written not for him alone, but also for us, to whom God will credit righteousness—for us who believe in him who raised Jesus our Lord from the dead."

HINTS FROM THE KITCHEN

- Belief in God is life-changing for middle school students and anyone else. In a world where taking a godly stand isn't always looked on favorably, believing in God's faithfulness and His many promises can strengthen their resolve to remain firm in their faith. These crosses serve as reminders of their belief in God.

- Before class, unwrap 10 or 15 colorful hard candies and place them in a resealable plastic bag. Squeeze the air out as you seal the bag. Put the bag on some thick fabric, felt, or thin foam over a solid and smooth surface. Gently break the candies into about three pieces each using a mallet, small hammer, or a rolling pin. Don't crush the candy too finely. However, do break the candy into smaller pieces for students who wear dental braces. Make one bag of crushed candy for each student, plus a few extra for visitors.

- The simplest way to portion out the corn syrup is to measure two spoonfuls using plastic spoons and place both filled spoons on a small paper plate for each student.

- The corn syrup will never dry completely, so students should place their candies as close together as possible.

- Have each student work on a paper plate the entire time to reduce stickiness on tables, etc.

- Wrap crosses in wax paper to prevent them from coming apart, or sticking to other items, if students take them home.

INGREDIENTS & SUPPLIES (SERVES 10)

- ❏ 4 lbs. colorful hard candies (about 10–15 candies per student)
- ❏ Corn syrup
- ❏ Resealable plastic bag (1 per student)
- ❏ Scissors
- ❏ Large paper plates (1 per student)
- ❏ Small paper plates (1 per student)
- ❏ Wax paper, 1 sheet no larger than 8 ½" x 11" per student (plus extra wax paper for wrapping completed project)
- ❏ Copy paper
- ❏ Plastic spoons (3 per student)
- ❏ Thick fabric, felt, or thin foam
- ❏ Mallet, small hammer, or rolling pin

CREATIVE COOKERY

ALLERGY WARNING: *It's possible that a student could be allergic to candy or corn syrup.*

Crosses will not look the same. Encourage students' creativity as they make their candy stained-glass crosses.

1. Give each student a bag of 20–30 pieces of colorful hard candy. (See Hints from the Kitchen for breaking the candy into pieces.)

2. Provide a large paper plate and an 8 ½" by 11" piece of wax paper for each student.

3. Hand out scissors and copy paper. Have the students cut a 2" by 4" cross out of the copy paper. They should then place the cross on the large paper plate and cover the cross and plate with the wax paper.

4. Give students two tablespoons of corn syrup on a small paper plate.

5. Encourage students to carefully drizzle the corn syrup onto their wax paper in the shape of the paper cross underneath.

6. Have students carefully place pieces of candy in the syrup over their crosses until all of the spaces are filled or they run out of candy.

7. Hand out plastic spoons for students to eat their crosses or allow the students to keep their stained-glass crosses. Cover entire plate with extra wax paper if transporting home. (Note: Corn syrup will not completely dry.)

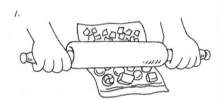

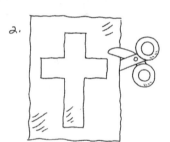

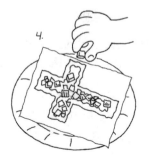

SAVOR IT!

Believing in God and His promises is a big part of the Christian life. For Abram, believing in God's promises meant trusting that God would give him a son even though he and his wife shouldn't have been able to have children.

- How does it feel to be asked to trust God for something you don't think is possible? *(frustrating, challenging, ridiculous, hopeful, encouraging, etc.)*

- What are some reasons Abram might have found it difficult to believe God's promise of a son? *(he and Sarai were older, they had waited a long time before God answered, etc.)*

- What are some things we believe about God that can help us during difficult times? *(Some answers might be that He saves us from our sin, He is powerful, He keeps His promises, He loves us, etc.)*

STAINED-GLASS CROSSES

Use your cross to share your belief in God's Son, Jesus.

RECIPE TO TAKE HOME

Ingredients:
- ❏ Colorful hard candies
- ❏ Corn syrup

Supplies:
- ❏ Resealable plastic bag
- ❏ Mallet, small hammer, or rolling pin
- ❏ Scissors
- ❏ Wax paper
- ❏ One large plate
- ❏ Plastic spoon

Directions:
1. Put 10–15 pieces of candy in a resealable plastic bag. Squeeze the air out of the bag as you seal it. Lay the bag of candy on a solid and smooth workspace covered with a thick piece of cloth or felt. Use a mallet, small hammer, or rolling pin to break each candy into two or three pieces.
2. Cut a cross out of wax paper. Place it on the large paper plate.
3. Measure out two tablespoons of corn syrup (using a plastic spoon).
4. Carefully spoon or drizzle the corn syrup over the wax-paper cross.
5. Carefully place the pieces of crushed candy on the cross until all of the spaces are filled.
6. When finished, eat the candy or save the cross to remind you that God calls us to believe in Him. (Note: Corn syrup will never completely dry.)

PERSEVERANCE ICE CREAM

PERSISTENCE PAYS IN MAKING THIS TREAT.

BIBLE BASIS:
Genesis 26:1–6, 12–25

MEMORY VERSE:
Cast your cares on the LORD and he will sustain you; he will never let the righteous fall. *Psalm 55:22*

BIBLE BACKGROUND

There was a famine in the land where Isaac and Rebekah lived. The Lord appeared to Isaac and said, "Do not go down to Egypt; live in the land where I tell you to live. Stay in this land for a while, and I will be with you and will bless you. For to you and your descendants I will give all these lands and will confirm the oath I swore to your father Abraham. I will make your descendants as numerous as the stars in the sky and will give them all these lands, and through your offspring all nations on earth will be blessed" (Gen. 26:2–4). So Isaac remained in Gerar, finding strength to persevere in God's promises. "Isaac planted crops in that land and the same year reaped a hundredfold, because the LORD blessed him" (Gen. 26:12).

Instead of giving up when there was no food, Isaac obeyed God and persevered in the midst of famine. As a result he rose from near starvation and destitution to one of the wealthiest men in the land. In fact, he became so wealthy that King Abimelech told him to, "Move away from us; you have become too powerful for us" (Gen. 26:16). God continued blessing Isaac's faithful perseverance and promised him once again, "I will bless you and will increase the number of your descendants for the sake of my servant Abraham" (Gen. 26:24). In response, Isaac built an altar to honor God. God was faithful to Isaac as he persevered in faith during adversity. Although God didn't take Isaac out of the difficult situation, He worked in and through the hardships empowering Isaac to persevere. Similarly, God promises to be with us, upholding us, as we persevere in doing good and following His instructions (Gal. 6:9). Holding on to that truth can bring us much-needed strength as we face the challenges of our own lives.

HINTS FROM THE KITCHEN

- Your students will practice perseverance today as they make ice cream in a zippered plastic bag.

- This edible project requires at least 10-15 minutes for students to toss, squeeze, and mush the bag enough to form the ice cream. Mixing the ingredients requires an additional five minutes.

- If time constraints exist, have students make the mix and squeeze their bags as they answer group questions. Allow time for eating the ice cream too.

- Rock salt (sometimes called ice cream salt) is available at most supermarkets or hardware stores. The rock salt lowers the temperature of the mixture to allow the cream to partially freeze.

- You can substitute table salt for rock salt, but you may need up to 1 cup of table salt to get the same effect as ½ cup of rock salt.

- Use a good-quality freezer bag with a secure zipper-type seal to assure salt water does not leak out of the bags. Resealable bags with a single-seal may not be secure enough.

- Place measuring cups and spoons on small paper plates to keep the workspace neat.

- Since the bags get rather cold to handle, consider providing mittens or gloves to make the kneading more comfortable. Alternately, wrapping the bag containing the ice in a towel before shaking and squeezing it may help.

INGREDIENTS & SUPPLIES
(SERVES 10)

- ❑ 10 gallon-size, plastic freezer bags with zipper seals (1 per student)
- ❑ 10 quart-size, plastic bags with zipper seals (1 per student)
- ❑ 25 cups of ice
- ❑ 5 cups of rock salt (½ cup per student) or 10 cups of table salt (1 cup per student)
- ❑ 5 cups whole milk, cream, or half and half (½ cup per student)
- ❑ 2 ½ teaspoons vanilla syrup (not vanilla extract, ¼ teaspoon per student)
- ❑ 10 tablespoons sugar (1 tablespoon per student)
- ❑ Optional: sliced fresh strawberries or strawberry preserves
- ❑ Measuring cups (1 cup and ½ cup)
- ❑ Measuring spoons (1 tablespoon, ¼ teaspoon)
- ❑ 10 plastic spoons (1 per student plus a few extra)
- ❑ Ice scoop

CREATIVE COOKERY

ALLERGY WARNING: *Some students could have milk or other dairy allergies. If so, they can use ½ cup fruit juice (per serving size) in the place of the milk, sugar, and syrup to make sorbet. Strawberries also can be an allergen, but are easily omitted.*

Making your own ice cream takes perseverance, but won't it be worth it?

1. For each student, carefully scoop 2 ½ cups of ice and ½ cup of rock salt into a gallon-sized, plastic freezer bag with a zipper seal.

2. Place the smaller quart-sized bag inside the large plastic bag and open it up. Fill the smaller bag with the ice cream ingredients: ½ cup milk, cream, or half and half; ¼ teaspoon vanilla syrup; 1 tablespoon sugar, and (optional) sliced fresh strawberries or 1 tablespoon strawberry preserves.

3. Zipper seal the inner bag first (double check that it is sealed), then zipper seal the outer bag containing ice and salt.

4. Gently shake, toss, and squish the plastic bag until the ice cream thickens. (This will take between 10 and 15 minutes.)

5. Unzip the large outer plastic bag and remove the small inner bag. Throw away the outer bag. Wipe the ice, salt, and water off the smaller plastic bag and then unzip it. Pray or have a volunteer pray to bless this special snack. Dip your spoon in and enjoy a cold treat!

SAVOR IT!

Isaac didn't have any crops. He was hungry and could have gone to Egypt and gotten food relatively quickly. Instead he persisted in following God's directions to stay in the place God wanted him to be. Then God abundantly blessed him, giving him wealth beyond anything he could have imagined. God rewarded Isaac's perseverance.

Perseverance is not always easy for us. We're used to getting things fast: fast food, drive-through convenience, microwave meals, instant potatoes, and three-minute macaroni and cheese. Waiting isn't easy, but God wants us to be persistent.

- **What are some things worth waiting for or persevering for?** (*Answers may include saving up for something you really want rather than spending the money on a cheap alternative, making good friends and keeping the friendship strong, continuing to do what God wants even when it's challenging, etc.*)

- **What's the hardest part about persevering for things?** (*Thinking you need something right away, discomfort like being hungry, wanting to do other things with the time, it might appear easier to give up, etc.*)

- **You probably aren't faced with a famine or people claiming your wells. But you do have your own hard things in life. What are some things in your life that require perseverance?** (*Allow students to share as they are comfortable.*)

PERSEVERANCE ICE CREAM

"Wow" your friends the next time they want ice cream but you can't get to the store . . . .

Ingredients:
- ❏ 2 ½ cups of ice and ½ cup of rock salt (up to 1 cup of table salt may be used to replace the rock salt)
- ❏ ½ cup milk, cream, or half and half
- ❏ ¼ teaspoon vanilla syrup (not vanilla extract)
- ❏ 1 tablespoon sugar
- ❏ Optional: fresh sliced strawberries or 1 tablespoon strawberry preserves

Supplies:
- ❏ 1 gallon-size, plastic freezer bag with zipper seal
- ❏ 1 quart-size, plastic bag with zipper seal
- ❏ ½ cup measuring cup
- ❏ ¼ teaspoon measuring spoon
- ❏ 1 tablespoon measuring spoon
- ❏ Spoon to eat the ice cream
- ❏ Small paper plate to catch spills

Directions:
1. Carefully place the ice and salt into the gallon-sized, plastic freezer bag with a secure zipper. (A zipper is a must for this recipe; resealable bags could leak.)
2. Insert the smaller, quart-sized bag into the large plastic bag and open it up. Fill with the ice cream ingredients: ½ cup milk, cream, or half and half; ¼ teaspoon vanilla syrup; 1 tablespoon sugar; and (optional) sliced fresh strawberries or 1 tablespoon strawberry preserves. Zipper seal inner bag first (double check it), then zipper seal outer bag containing ice and salt.
3. Gently shake, squeeze, and squish your plastic bag until the ice cream thickens. (This part will take between 10 and 15 minutes.)
4. Unzip the large outer plastic bag and remove the small inner bag. Throw away the outer bag. Wipe the ice, salt, and water off of the smaller plastic bag and then unzip it. Enjoy your frozen treat!

FRIENDSHIP BREAD

LEARN THE ART OF "SMOOSHING" AND MAKE BREAD AT THE SAME TIME.

BIBLE BASIS:
Genesis 27:1–24, 30, 41

MEMORY VERSE:
And whatever you do, whether in word or deed, do it all in name of the Lord Jesus.
Colossians 3:17a

BIBLE BACKGROUND

Family members may disagree from time to time . . . but hopefully not to the extent of Jacob and Esau. These brothers fought from the moment they left their mother's womb (Gen. 25:25–26) until they were grown men. In Genesis 25, Jacob deviously talked his brother into selling his birthright. Esau held what should have been of great value in low esteem, and sold his birthright for a meal. Neither brother honored the other and they both paid for this throughout their lives.

As firstborn, Esau was also entitled to his father Isaac's blessing. This blessing would be passed from Esau to his firstborn son, and so on through the generations. Instead Jacob obtained the blessing fraudulently. Losing this blessing affected not only Esau but also his lineage. Even though Jacob gained the birthright through deceit (Gen. 27:34–35), he inherited the promise foretold to his mother Rachel. Jacob, not Esau, would continue the chosen lineage and prosper in the future. However, initially, instead of enjoying this blessing in the presence of his family, Jacob lived in fear of his brother Esau. Jacob fled from his brother and lived far from his parents.

Honoring God in all relationships means looking out for the good of others before your own good. These brothers didn't do that. Instead, they selfishly brought ruin onto their family for a time.

HINTS FROM THE KITCHEN

- Today's edible project differs from the others in this book, but should be great fun for the students. They will make *starter* for friendship bread. (*Starter* is a dough made in advance that helps the bread to rise.) The *starter* needs tender loving care, but if directions are carefully followed, it will "grow" into many new *starters* for students to pass on to friends and family, who in turn can pass it on.

- To reduce costs, request that each student bring his or her own packet of yeast. However, have a few packets on hand for visitors or students who don't remember to bring the yeast.

- Students will mix ingredients today, then over time will add to the ingredients, knead the *starter*, and release the air built up in the bags. After 10 days they will have extra *starter* that can either be frozen or given away with directions for making more *starter* and friendship bread.

- You'll need warm milk and warm water. Some options if there is not a microwave, hot plate, or hot water source near your classroom include:

OPTION 1: At home, bring milk and water to a boil (each student will need 1 cup of milk and ¼ cup of water) and carefully pour them into thermoses. Milk needs to be 110 degrees so even if it cools some, it will be warm enough to use for the recipe. Water, too, just needs to be warm. In the classroom use a coffee maker to heat water and an espresso maker and metal canister to steam milk.

OPTION 2: Make the *starter* 10 days ahead and divide up among your students (1 cup of *starter* per student). (Instead of beginning at Day 1, students would begin at Day 10).

INGREDIENTS & SUPPLIES
(SERVES 10)

- ❑ 10 gallon-size, zippered freezer bags (1 per student)
- ❑ Permanent marker
- ❑ 10 pkgs. dry yeast (1 package per student)
- ❑ 2 ½ cups warm water (¼ cup per student)
- ❑ 10 cups all-purpose flour (1 cup per student)
- ❑ 10 cups white granulated sugar (1 cup per student)
- ❑ 10 cups warm milk heated to 110 degrees (1 cup per student)
- ❑ Plastic or wooden bowls—cannot be metal (1 per student)
- ❑ Plastic or wooden spoons—cannot be metal (1 per student)

CREATIVE COOKERY

ALLERGY WARNING: Check for allergies before giving students the starter *and Recipe to Take Home.*

Give a gift that keeps on giving!

1. In a plastic or wooden bowl, mix one package dry yeast, ¼ cup warm water, 1 cup all-purpose flour, 1 cup white granulated sugar, and 1 cup warm milk. This is your bread *starter*.

2. Transfer the *starter* to a gallon-size, zippered bag. If possible, keep the *starter* in the plastic or glass bowl until small bubbles form, then transfer to plastic bag. This completes Day 1 of the recipe.

Send the following instructions home with students:

Day 1: Make *starter* and keep at room temperature in the gallon-size, zippered plastic bag. (This was done today in class.)

To Do at Home:
Days 2–4: Each day, open the bag a bit to let out excess air, then reseal the bag and knead the *starter*.

Day 5: Add 1 cup sugar, 1 cup flour, and 1 cup milk to bag. (Milk can be cold.) Squeeze air out as you reseal the bag and knead until smooth.

Days 6–9: Each day open the bag to let out excess air, then reseal the bag and knead the *starter*, as on days 2–4.

Day 10: Add 1 cup sugar, 1 cup flour, and 1 cup milk. (Again, milk can be cold.) Knead until smooth. Use one cup of this *starter* to make the Friendship Bread Recipe. Divide the rest of the *starter* into one-cup

portions in new gallon-size, zippered bags. Each bag becomes another batch of *starter*. Date each bag. Consider these bags Day 1 of new 10-day cycle. Pass them on (with new dates) as Day 1 with To Do at Home directions plus the Friendship Bread Recipe. Although *starter* doesn't need to be refrigerated or frozen while it's being made, once *starter* is at Day 10, bake it immediately, give it away, refrigerate it for short-term use, or freeze it. (Note: *Starter* can be frozen in one-cup quantities. Frozen *starter* requires at least three hours to thaw before using. *Starter* should be used within three months.)

SAVOR IT!

Jacob and Esau didn't honor each other the way they should have. Instead of working as a team, they constantly fought and competed with one another. Relationships are complicated because we live in a sinful world. However, God calls us to please Him in all our relationships. Take time this week to honor someone.

- **What happened when Jacob and Esau refused to honor each other?** *(they lost the friendship brothers should have, their future families were impacted, etc.)*

- **What's one way you have honored a family member?** *(by not arguing with them, by doing chores before asked, etc.)*

- **Why do you think God wants us to honor others in our relationships?** *(all people are important to God; when we honor others, we let them know that they are special and appreciated, etc.)*

FRIENDSHIP BREAD RECIPE

RECIPE TO TAKE HOME

*ALLERGY WARNING: *Be sure your friends are aware of the ingredients in this friendship bread before you pass it on.*
Make some friendship bread to eat and some to pass along. (One of the main ingredients is *starter*, prepped to Day 10 in the At Home directions. *Starter* is a dough you make ahead that helps the bread rise.)

Ingredients:
- ❏ 1 cup *starter*
- ❏ ⅔ cup vegetable oil
- ❏ 3 eggs
- ❏ 2 cups all-purpose flour
- ❏ 1 cup white granulated sugar
- ❏ 1 teaspoon ground cinnamon
- ❏ ½ teaspoon baking soda
- ❏ ½ teaspoon salt
- ❏ 1 ¼ teaspoons baking powder
- ❏ 1 teaspoon vanilla extract
- ❏ Optional: 1 cup raisins or chocolate chips

Supplies:
- ❏ 2 greased 9" x 5" loaf pans
- ❏ Spoon for mixing ingredients (Any spoon is fine; metal can only not be used when first mixing with yeast.)

Directions:
1. Preheat oven to 350 degrees.
2. Grease two 9" x 5" loaf pans.
3. In a large bowl, combine the *starter* with oil, eggs, flour, sugar, cinnamon, baking soda, salt, baking powder, vanilla, and the optional raisins or chocolate chips. Mix well.
4. Pour into loaf pans.
5. Bake in preheated oven for 50–60 minutes. (If you aren't used to baking, have an adult assist you with the oven when baking this recipe.)

FRUIT PIZZA

A WALL OF SWEET FRUIT ... WHO WOULDN'T WANT THAT?

BIBLE BASIS:
Genesis 33:1–11

MEMORY VERSE:
Bear with each other and forgive whatever grievances you may have against one another. Forgive as the Lord forgave you.
Colossians 3:13

BIBLE BACKGROUND

Jacob and Esau had a chance to reconcile and forgive each another. They could have put past differences aside and loved each other as brothers should. At this point, so much time had passed that they were grown and had their own families, servants, and possessions. But while some efforts were made toward reconciliation and forgiveness, later chapters in Genesis show that some issues apparently remained between the two. Jacob refused to travel with Esau, would not let Esau's men accompany him as was his brother's desire, and finally lied about wanting to meet up with his brother later on.

Years later the consequences of this lack of full reconciliation between the brothers revealed itself through Jacob and Esau's descendants. Jacob settled down in an area called Succoth away from Esau. Esau finally settled in Seir and became the father of the Edomites (Gen. 36:8–9). For centuries after the initial fight between brothers, the two regions remained enemies.

Sadly, the only thing Genesis records that the two brothers did together after the meeting noted in Genesis 33 was to bury their father, Isaac (Gen. 35:29).

How tragic for a family unit that could have done great things together had it known the power of forgiveness. Instead of tearing down walls of bitterness, they allowed them to remain and generations after them paid as a result. For forgiveness to tear down walls and bring healing, we must be able to truly accept the forgiveness of others, fully forgive others, and be willing to build upon the trust needed for healthy relationships.

HINTS FROM THE KITCHEN

🍽 Real-life examples serve as valuable learning tools. During today's lesson, share examples from your life that show giving and receiving forgiveness.

🍽 Have students give a piece of the fruit pizza to a family member. Prepare enough of the cookie crust, if possible, for each student to enjoy a piece in class and take one home to another family member. As an option, have decorative or colorful plates and plastic wrap available for the take-home treat. Bring blank cards and envelopes—or colorful construction paper—and pens so students can jot a quick note to the family member. Encourage students to let this be a reminder to reach out to family members in love.

🍽 Square or rectangular-shaped pans can be used instead of the round pizza pan.

🍽 When cutting the pizza, only the teacher should use the knife or pizza cutter.

🍽 Use this opportunity to get your students thinking honestly about how willing they are to forgive others, and how ready they are to accept forgiveness from people they hurt.

INGREDIENTS & SUPPLIES
(SERVES 10)

- ❏ One 16 oz. pkg. refrigerated sugar-cookie dough, pre-baked (see instructions that follow)
- ❏ Round pizza pan or cookie sheet
- ❏ Rolling pin
- ❏ Spatula
- ❏ One 8 oz. pkg. whipped cream, cream cheese, or white frosting
- ❏ At least 4 cups of any combination of grapes, strawberries, blueberries, blackberries, peeled and sliced banana, kiwi fruit slices (rinds removed), canned fruit, etc.
- ❏ Knife or pizza cutter
- ❏ Paper plates (1 per student)
- ❏ Plastic wrap
- ❏ Optional: blank note cards and envelopes (1 each per student) or construction paper, note/recipe cards, and pens
- ❏ Optional: clear tape
- ❏ Optional: decorative or colorful paper plates
- ❏ Optional: colorful plastic wrap

CREATIVE COOKERY

ALLERGY WARNING: Strawberries can be an allergen, but are easily omitted. For students with wheat allergies, create a small "crustless" pizza on a plate. If a student has dairy allergies, replace the cream cheese or whipped cream with a non-dairy whipped topping or dairy-free frosting.

Build a wall of fruit "pizza." As you eat it, tear it down and remember that forgiveness tears down walls.

1. Prior to class, roll the refrigerated sugar-cookie dough into a pizza shape with a rolling pin. Place the dough on a pan or pizza stone. Bake the dough according to package directions. Allow this large cookie "crust" to cool completely before wrapping the cookie on the pan with plastic wrap.

2. Have students use a spatula to lightly cover the cookie/"pizza" with whipped cream, cream cheese, or white frosting. (Divide large groups into smaller groups based on how many pizza crusts were created.)

3. Allow students to decorate the pizza with various fruits.

4. Cut the pizza for the students, or if using the optional plan to share with family, divide into enough equal-sized pieces so each student can eat one piece and take one home.

5. Pray, thanking God for the fruit pizza. Enjoy.

6. Refrigerate any extra pieces of the fruit pizza.

SAVOR IT!

People of all ages struggle to forgive at times, but it's an area that God expects us to grow, and He'll help us with it. Understanding and accepting Jesus' forgiveness of everything we do wrong, when we ask Him, certainly is a good first step. Prayer is another means with which God can break down the walls in our hearts that keep us from offering forgiveness to others and accepting it too. When you want to hold on to hurts, remember all that Jesus has forgiven you.

- Why do you think it's so hard for us, like Esau and Jacob, to say and mean the words, "I'm sorry" and "I forgive you"? *(pride, a desire to hold on to hurt, thinking I have good reasons for being upset, doing things so bad I can't forgive myself, etc.)*

- When have you seen forgiveness tear down walls between people, and what happened? *(Allow time for sharing.)*

- Is there someone you have offended and need to ask to forgive you, or someone that you need to forgive? Don't hold on to it any longer. Call, e-mail, or visit with this person today and put "unforgiveness" behind you.

FRUIT PIZZA

Build up this "pizza" with a wall of fruit. As you eat it, tear it down and remember that's what forgiveness does. When you forgive, it tastes sweet as well!

Ingredients:
- ❑ One 16 oz. package refrigerated sugar-cookie dough
- ❑ One 8 oz. pkg. whipped cream, cream cheese, or white frosting (enough to thinly cover the cookie)
- ❑ 4 cups of any combination of grapes, strawberries, blueberries, blackberries, kiwi, banana, or canned fruit

Supplies:
- ❑ Pizza pan or cookie sheet
- ❑ Rolling pin
- ❑ Spatula
- ❑ Paper plates
- ❑ Plastic wrap
- ❑ Optional: clear tape
- ❑ Optional: decorative or colorful paper plates
- ❑ Optional: cards/envelopes, colorful construction paper pieces, index/recipe cards
- ❑ Optional: colorful plastic wrap

Directions:
1. Use a rolling pin to roll all the cookie dough into a pizza shape. Carefully place on a pizza pan or baking sheet.
2. Ask an adult to help you bake the large cookie according to the package directions or until cookie "pizza" crust is cooked through and firm.
3. Let the cookie cool, then use a spatula to lightly cover cookie with whipped cream, cream cheese, or white frosting.
4. Decorate fruit pizza with various fruits.
5. Have an adult help you cut the fruit pizza into pieces. Eat and share with others. Refrigerate any leftovers.
6. Optional: Decorate recipe cards and then put pieces of your fruit pizza on colorful paper plates covered with plastic wrap. Give cards and fruit pizza to others.

COLORFUL KABOBS | VEGGIES NEVER LOOKED SO GOOD.

BIBLE BASIS:
Genesis 49:29—50:21

MEMORY VERSE:
And we know that in all things God works for the good of those who love him, who have been called according to his purpose.
Romans 8:28

BIBLE BACKGROUND

Joseph had many reasons to doubt God's control in his life. As a boy, his brothers disliked him because their father, Jacob, favored Joseph and because of the superiority implied by his dreams. He was thrown in a pit and sold into slavery in Egypt by his own brothers. Then he was sent to prison in Egypt despite having done the right thing and fighting off the advances of his master's wife. Many people in Joseph's situation might have denounced God's sovereignty. Not Joseph. As a result of his faith in God's control over his life, "the LORD was with Joseph and gave him success in whatever he did" (Gen. 39:23b).

Throughout this difficult time, Joseph kept his circumstances in perspective. As a young teen he had dreamed that he would rule over his brothers (Gen. 37:5–11). Although this didn't happen until later in his life, it did eventually occur. Joseph's family bowed down before him, and his brothers begged for his forgiveness. Joseph had already forgiven his brothers, so he readily invited them back into his life, providing food and a safe haven for them during the famine (Gen. 45:1–7).

After Joseph's father Jacob died, the brothers suddenly feared Joseph again. "What if Joseph holds a grudge against us and pays us back for all the wrongs we did to him?" (Gen. 50:15). The brothers asked Joseph for forgiveness once more. Joseph wept and said, "You intended to harm me, but God intended it for good to accomplish what is now being done . . . So then, don't be afraid. I will provide for you and your children" (Gen. 50:20–21a).

Joseph trusted God's control over his life and saw many lives saved and his family restored. We too can trust God and know that He is in control and will accomplish His plans.

HINTS FROM THE KITCHEN

- Use the vegetable kabobs as an analogy of God's control. Explain to students that even when things in life seem out of control, God holds everything together. The different vegetables on the kabob stick can represent various challenges in life. But it's the stick that holds them together, keeping things from falling apart. God is the stick, and He's in control. No matter what issues surround us, God holds our life securely in His hands. His control gives us assurance and reminds us of His love for us.

- If the ranch dressing is opened, keep it in a cooler or gallon-size plastic bag with ice. Most ranch dressings do not need refrigeration prior to opening, but check the label.

INGREDIENTS & SUPPLIES
(SERVES 10)

- ❏ 3 medium green, red, or yellow peppers (or all 3)
- ❏ 2 medium broccoli or cauliflower heads (raw)
- ❏ 2 medium cucumbers, peeled and sliced into thick, round pieces
- ❏ Two 6 oz. cans whole, pitted black olives
- ❏ Disposable wooden bamboo skewers or reusable metal skewers (1 per student)
- ❏ Plastic containers or resealable plastic bags (1 per student)
- ❏ One 16 oz. container ranch dressing
- ❏ Paper plates (1 per student)
- ❏ Can opener
- ❏ Vegetable or potato peeler
- ❏ Bowl
- ❏ Serving spoons

CREATIVE COOKERY

ALLERGY WARNING: *If you have a chef with dairy allergies, substitute Italian dressing for the ranch dressing.*

God holds your life together. He's in control. This skewer holds all of these vegetables together too. Dip these healthy veggies into ranch dressing and enjoy a crunchy snack.

1. Prior to class, carefully wash the peppers, broccoli, cauliflower, and cucumbers. Dry with a paper towel. With a knife, cut apart the peppers and remove the seeds. Peel the cucumber and cut the other vegetables to fit onto the skewers. Place similar vegetables together in plastic containers or resealable plastic bags.

2. Allow student volunteers to open the can(s) of olives, drain excess water into a sink, and then place the olives in a bowl.

3. Spread comtainers or bags filled with the vegetables on a table and provide serving spoons so students can serve themselves.

4. Set out disposable wooden bamboo skewers or reusable metal skewers on the table.

5. Encourage students to come to the table to make their skewers of vegetables.

6. Offer ranch dressing for dipping.

7. Pray or have a volunteer pray, asking God to bless the food.

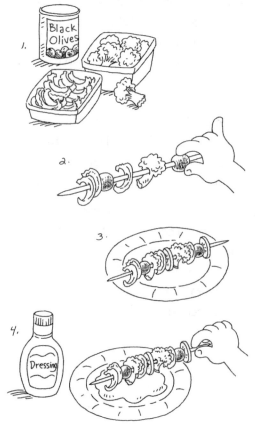

SAVOR IT!

Joseph's life was not easy. He faced difficulties with every turn. Yet he never wavered in his faith in God and remained confident that God was in control of his life—from his childhood dreams to his rule under Pharaoh. Even when he was wrongly accused and thrown in jail, Joseph continued to serve God and his character never suffered. We too can rest assured that God is in control of our lives. No matter what happens, our future is secure in Him.

- **What were some circumstances in Joseph's life when God might not have seemed in control?** *(He was sold into slavery, he was wrongly accused, and he was placed in jail.)*

- **How did God show He was in control?** *(If these difficult things hadn't happened, Joseph wouldn't have risen to power and been able to save his family from famine.)*

- **What are some areas in our lives where we can trust that God is in control?** *(Allow students to share. Consider sharing an example from your own life.)*

VEGETABLE KABOBS

God is the "stick" holding your life together. He's in control. This skewer holds all of these vegetables together. Dip these healthy veggies into ranch dressing and enjoy a crunchy snack.

Ingredients:
- ❑ 1 small green, red, or yellow pepper (or portions of all 3)
- ❑ Raw broccoli or cauliflower heads
- ❑ 1 small cucumber, peeled and sliced into thick, round pieces
- ❑ One 6 oz. can whole, pitted black olives
- ❑ Ranch dressing

Supplies:
- ❑ Disposable wooden bamboo skewers or reusable metal skewers
- ❑ Paper plates
- ❑ Can opener
- ❑ Vegetable or potato peeler
- ❑ Napkins

Directions:
1. Wash the pepper, broccoli or cauliflower, and cucumber in running water. Dry with a paper towel. Have an adult help you use a knife to carefully cut apart the peppers and remove the seeds from the inside. Peel the cucumber and cut the other vegetables so they'll fit onto the skewers.
2. Open the can of olives and drain excess water into a sink.
3. Create vegetable kabobs by placing vegetables on skewers.
4. Dip in ranch dressing.
5. Store any unused vegetables in resealable plastic containers or bags in the refrigerator.
6. Refrigerate any leftover ranch dressing.

RECIPE TO TAKE HOME

GREAT GUIDES

SWEET SCROLLS FORETOLD.

BIBLE BASIS:
Exodus 19:1–8,
20; 20:1–3

MEMORY VERSE:
All Scripture is God-
breathed and is useful
for teaching, rebuking,
correcting and training
in righteousness.
2 Timothy 3:16

BIBLE BACKGROUND

Three months after the Israelites left Egypt, they waited, camped in the Sinai desert. God had planned for His people, the Israelites, to receive the Ten Commandments at this time. Instead of just telling them what He expected of them directly or shouting His laws over the mountain for all the people to hear, God worked through Moses to deliver these important rules.

In Moses' first meeting with God on Mt. Sinai, God explained what He expected of His people. God reminded them of how He saved them from the Egyptians, as if "on eagles' wings." He also assured them, "I . . . brought you to myself" (Exod. 19:4).

God promised Moses that if the people kept His commandments He would make them His "treasured possession," "a kingdom of priests," and "a holy nation" (Exod. 19:5–6). Moses conveyed these truths to the Israelites before they received God's commandments. After he spoke to them, Moses went once again to the top of Mt. Sinai. Moses reported to God that the people said they would obey Him fully. At this time God gave Moses the Ten Commandments.

God gave His laws to the Israelites to guide and instruct them, and His laws have been given to guide and instruct us as well. His rules can help us navigate the difficulties of this world. They aren't there to keep us from having fun; actually, quite the opposite! They help keep us pure so we can enjoy the abundant life God offers. Trust the Bible to guide you; seek and follow God's instructions and you will not end up lost and wandering.

HINTS FROM THE KITCHEN

🍴 For today's project students will make edible scrolls from large flour tortillas. Point out that while God wrote the Ten Commandments on stone tablets, most of Scripture was originally written on scrolls, and these yummy snacks remind us that God's Word is the best guide to follow in life.

🍴 Remind students not to make the scrolls too heavy. They should lightly spread their cream cheese on the tortilla. This will enable the tortillas to roll up better and stay tied together.

INGREDIENTS & SUPPLIES
(SERVES 10)

- ❏ 10 large flour tortillas (1 per student)
- ❏ 8 oz. tub whipped or regular cream cheese (about 2 tablespoons per student)
- ❏ ¾ cup cinnamon sugar (1 tablespoon + 2 teaspoons cinnamon mixed with ½ cup + 2 tablespoons white granulated sugar)
- ❏ 1 container colorful sprinkles
- ❏ 1 small bag black or red thin licorice ropes
- ❏ Large plates (1 per student)
- ❏ Plastic knives (1 per student)
- ❏ Plastic bowls
- ❏ Plastic spoons (1 per student)
- ❏ Optional: resealable plastic bags

CREATIVE COOKERY

***ALLERGY WARNING:** If you have a chef with dairy allergies, substitute a dairy-free margarine for the cream cheese. For wheat allergies, corn tortillas may be an alternative, but be sure to ask.*

These edible scrolls are rolled together with goodness, just like the contents of God's Word.

1. Ahead of time, make the cinnamon sugar mixture and place it in a bowl. Fill another bowl with sprinkles and place both bowls on the table. Each bowl should have its own spoon.

2. Open the packaging for the remaining ingredients and arrange each on plates on the table where students can access them easily.

3. Have students spread cream cheese on their tortillas, dust with cinnamon sugar mixture, and cover with sprinkles as desired.

4. Have students roll both sides of the tortillas toward each other until they touch, forming a scroll.

5. Tie scrolls with licorice rope.

6. The scrolls can be eaten or saved in resealable plastic bags. Praying before eating will remind the students to be thankful.

SAVOR IT!

The Bible is God's gift to us, loaded with loving instructions. We can find guidance for any situation there. God's Word overflows with verses on love, helping others, obeying and pleasing God, caring for the sick and needy, and just about anything we might encounter in life.

- When do (or can) you read your Bible and have your prayer and devotional time? *(Have students share. Day or night or in-between, there is no such thing as a wrong time to read God's Word.)*

- Where do you look for guidance? Why did you choose those things? *(Let students discuss their ideas.)*

- What are some times we can look to God's Word for guidance? *(when we are afraid, when we don't know what to do, when we want to learn to please God, etc.)*

EDIBLE SCROLLS

These edible scrolls are filled with goodness, just like the contents of God's Word.

RECIPE TO TAKE HOME

Ingredients:
- ❑ 1 large flour tortilla
- ❑ 2 tablespoons cream cheese
- ❑ Cinnamon sugar (½ teaspoon cinnamon mixed with 3 teaspoons white granulated sugar)
- ❑ Colorful sprinkles (as desired)
- ❑ Black or red thin licorice rope

Supplies:
- ❑ Large plate
- ❑ Plastic knife
- ❑ Plastic bowl
- ❑ Plastic spoon

Directions:
1. Take the tortilla and lay it open on a large plate.
2. Make the cinnamon sugar mixture in a bowl by mixing the cinnamon and sugar.
3. Spread cream cheese over the tortilla.
4. Dust with cinnamon sugar.
5. Cover with sprinkles as desired.
6. Roll both sides of the tortilla toward the other until they touch (forming a scroll).
7. Tie the scroll with licorice rope.

ANGELIC SUBSTANCE

ANGEL-SHAPED SANDWICHES WITH FILLERS GALORE!

BIBLE BASIS:
Matthew 1:18–21

MEMORY VERSE:
Salvation is found in no one else, for there is no other name under heaven given to men by which we must be saved. *Acts 4:12*

BIBLE BACKGROUND

When Joseph learned that Mary was pregnant he likely felt betrayed. He was a godly man, however, so he planned to handle the matter quietly and in a gentle way so that Mary would not be punished. In their day, an unfaithful woman could be stoned to death (as seen with the woman in John 8). After Joseph considered how he would respond, an angel appeared to Joseph in a dream. The angel told him that Mary had not been unfaithful and that he should take Mary as his wife because the child in her womb was the promised Messiah. The angel even told Joseph what to name the baby—Jesus, which means "the Lord saves."

Joseph did as the Lord commanded (Matt. 1:24). Joseph showed his love for Mary and his faith that God would keep His promises (Isa. 7:14 prophesied the virgin birth). Joseph must have realized that God was allowing him to be a part of a magnificent work: God was made flesh (John 1:14a) and became a Savior for sinners. Joseph would be Jesus' earthly father, teaching and guiding Him through His young years. Quite a responsibility, given Joseph was raising the child who became the Savior of the world! As Acts 4:12 says, "Salvation is found in no one else, for there is no other name under heaven given to men by which we must be saved." This baby to come would be the One who saves.

HINTS FROM THE KITCHEN

- Today, students will enjoy making sandwiches in lesson-related shapes using angel and nativity scene cookie cutters.

- If you don't have Christmas-themed cookie cutters, they can be purchased at many craft stores, kitchen stores, and grocery stores (check the specialty aisles). You might also borrow angel-shaped or nativity scene cookie cutters from friends so you have several cookie cutters to speed the process.

- Consider setting small bowls of sandwich fillings on a turntable or two for students to spin around. Fillings also can be placed in bowls on round or long tables that students can maneuver around.

- Bring at least three fillers but don't feel like you have to provide all the suggested selections. These are listed as ideas only. Avoid peanut butter in case you have any people with nut allergies in your group.

- The supply list includes a cooler with ice, which is recommended to transport perishable foods from home to keep them chilled and fresh for the students.

INGREDIENTS & SUPPLIES (SERVES 10)

- ❑ 1-2 loaves of white, wheat, sourdough, or raisin bread (2 slices per student)
- ❑ Sandwich fillings (choose at least 3): lunch meats, cheeses, cream cheese (plain or flavored), cinnamon sugar, jams, and condiments
- ❑ Several angel-shaped or other appropriate nativity-scene cookie cutters
- ❑ Clean cloths or paper towels
- ❑ Cooler filled with ice or ice packs
- ❑ A long or large round table or turntable or two
- ❑ Paper plates (1 per student)
- ❑ Plastic spoons and knives

CREATIVE COOKERY

ALLERGY WARNING: *For chefs with wheat allergies, corn tortillas may be an alternative to the bread (but be sure to ask). For chefs who are allergic to dairy products, you might substitute dairy-free mayonnaise or margarine.*

Instead of another trip through the salad bar, think sandwich bar! Grab some tasty bread, cut it into an angel or nativity-scene shape, and top with your favorite sandwich filler. Don't be afraid to try something new!

1. Arrange bread, cookie cutters, and other supplies, plus plates of sandwich fillings, on tables as a sandwich bar for students to make their sandwiches.

2. Let students select their cookie cutters and show how to cover them with cloth or paper towels to protect their hands before pressing the cutters through two slices of bread. It may help to cut one slice at a time.

3. Have students select their favorite fillers from the sandwich bar to make sandwiches in shapes we associate with a celebration of Jesus' birth.

4. After all students have made their sandwiches, pray or ask for a volunteer to ask God to bless the food.

SAVOR IT!

Joseph and Mary found themselves in an extraordinary situation: becoming parents to the Savior of the world. It took great courage for them to take on this task. They probably felt humbled and the responsibility may have been difficult for them at times. God purposefully gave Jesus to Mary and Joseph to care for and nurture Him as He grew. Jesus came to this earth to save us from our sins. We can rejoice that Jesus was born to save!

- **How do you think Joseph felt when he realized that his bride-to-be was expecting a baby?** *(confused, angry, betrayed, etc.)* **How might Mary have felt?** *(scared, excited, hopeful, etc.)*

- **What events in the story confirmed that Jesus was to be the Savior of the world?** *(angels said so, prophecy was fulfilled, etc.)*

- **What other events then and since Jesus' birth confirm that He is the Savior?** *(Allow time for answers and discussion. Answers might include miracles, the resurrection, or experiences in your life and your students' lives.)*

ANGELIC SUBSTANCE

*ALLERGY WARNING: *Avoid any food items such as peanut butter or dairy, if anyone has food allergies.*

Next time it's your turn to make lunch or dinner for your friends or family, try this sandwich bar idea. Since everyone can choose their own fillings you're bound to have a happy crowd!

RECIPE TO TAKE HOME:

Ingredients:
- ❑ Bread (your selection of white, wheat, sourdough, raisin, rye, or other varieties)
- ❑ Sandwich fillings (choose at least 3) such as lunch meats, cheeses, cream cheese (plain or flavored), cinnamon sugar, jams, and condiments. *Note: Keep items needing refrigeration cool until ready to use.

Supplies:
- ❑ Plates
- ❑ Clean cloths or paper towels
- ❑ Angel-shaped or other nativity-scene cookie cutters
- ❑ Plastic spoons
- ❑ Plastic knives

Directions:
1. Choose several of your favorite kinds of bread and sandwich fillings to satisfy your guests and yourself.
2. Just before time to eat, bring out the ingredients and supplies to arrange them on a table.
3. Have your guests or family use cookie cutters to cut shapes from bread slices. Place a clean cloth or paper towel over the cookie cutter to protect hands from sharp edges on cookie cutters as you press firmly down on the bread.
4. Have your guests or family make their own sandwiches.
5. Sit down together. Thank the Lord for the food. Eat and enjoy time together celebrating the Savior's birth!

REFRESHINGLY BLUE | SIP AWAY THE WATER BLUE.

BIBLE BASIS:
Matthew 3:13–17

MEMORY VERSE:
You are all sons of God through faith in Christ Jesus, for all of you who were baptized into Christ have clothed yourselves with Christ.
Galatians 3:26–27

BIBLE BACKGROUND

John the Baptist hesitated to baptize Jesus because he knew who Jesus was: the Son of God. John humbly questioned Jesus' request. After all, Jesus was the One—the Son of God—whom John had been proclaiming all along. Now John wasn't exactly sure what his role should be. Jesus, however, wanted to be baptized, in large part because it would proclaim to the world that He was ready for business! Jesus' teaching and healing ministry was about to begin, and He wanted those who had come to John seeking the Messiah to know that He had come.

As John baptized Jesus, he witnessed something powerful—the Trinity at work on this earth. God the Father spoke from heaven; God the Son went up out of the water; and God the Holy Spirit descended like a dove. What a spectacular experience and blessing for John who had spent his life to this point waiting for a Savior, Israel's redeemer. Jesus' baptism marked the beginning of His messianic ministry. John proclaimed the kingdom was near (Matt. 3:2), and now, what God foretold through John and the prophets was here.

Baptism is one way we identify with Christ and is a distinguishing mark. When a person is baptized, the act indicates a special relationship. That person assumes a unique identity and a special family—the Church. If possible have a leader from your church share about baptism with your group.

HINTS FROM THE KITCHEN

- Today, create a colorful drink—a blue drink to be exact! This project offers leeway depending on whether it is easier for you to provide a large punch bowl or a blender for making individual drinks. Both recipe options are provided.

- If making individual drinks, students may help make their own. This allows one-on-one time with each student.

- Instead of blue food coloring, use a blue-colored fruit drink or sports drink. If using the punch bowl, the entire group can participate. Some students can pour in the soft drink; others can drop in the blue food coloring while others add fresh blueberries and scoops of vanilla ice cream. If possible serve the drinks in clear plastic cups to highlight the color.

INGREDIENTS & SUPPLIES (SERVES 10)

- ❏ 10 cups of ice (1 cup per student to use only if using a blender)
- ❏ Two 2-liter bottles of clear carbonated soda (use for punch bowl and blender)
- ❏ A few drops of blue food coloring (use for punch bowl and blender)
- ❏ 1 cup of blueberries (if using the punch bowl they could float on top; if using the blender, mix in about 10 blueberries per person)
- ❏ 10 clear, tall, plastic cups (1 per student)
- ❏ Large spoon
- ❏ Straws or plastic spoons for students who may wish to use them
- ❏ Optional: 2 cups vanilla ice cream (use only for the punch bowl)
- ❏ Punch bowl or blender

CREATIVE COOKERY

ALLERGY WARNING: *Although the ingredients used today should not be allergens, some students may not be able to have too much sugar or could be lactose intolerant and unable to have ice cream mixed into their drink. Omit for those students.*

Refreshingly Blue. That's what these drinks are for you!

1. For blended drinks: Allow students to help combine 1 cup of ice; 1 serving of clear, carbonated soda; a few drops of blue food coloring (or mix in 1 serving of other blue-colored drink); and 10 blueberries in a blender. Blend until all items are thoroughly mixed, about 30 seconds. Pour into a clear glass and serve. Rinse out blender as needed with warm water.

2. For punch bowl drinks: Students can help pour the clear, carbonated soda; a few drops of blue food coloring (or necessary servings of other blue-colored drink); 1 cup of blueberries; and 2 cups vanilla ice cream (if desired), into the bowl. They should then mix it all together with a large spoon. Serve in clear, plastic cups. Have students line up and either serve themselves the drink or have one volunteer serve everyone.

3. Provide straws or plastic spoons for students who may wish to use them.

SAVOR IT!

When Jesus was baptized in the blue waters of the Jordan River, He formally began His ministry. Jesus wanted to publicly announce who He was and that He was ready to impact the world. John the Baptist had firsthand knowledge of Jesus, was His relative, and even proclaimed His coming. Yet John was just as amazed as everyone else at the events surrounding Jesus' baptism. It must have been a very joyous thing for John to behold the Messiah he had spent so much time proclaiming. Remember Jesus' baptism whenever you make today's refreshing blue drinks at home.

- How does your church carry out baptisms? *(Answers will vary.)*

- Why do you think Jesus chose to be baptized? *(to make His ministry public, to do what His Father in heaven desired, to give Himself and others a starting point to Jesus' adult ministry, etc.)*

- What does your baptism mean to you? *(Let your students respond. They might say identifying with Christ, showing myself as part of the church, representing death to sin, starting a special kind of life, etc.)*

REFRESHINGLY BLUE

Next time you crave a refreshing drink, why go for the ordinary? Make this refreshingly blue drink and remember Jesus' amazing baptism!

Ingredients:
- ❏ 1 cup of ice per person (if using a blender)
- ❏ Clear, carbonated soda (one 2-liter bottle will serve 4–6 people)
- ❏ A few drops of blue food coloring (use for punch bowl, blender, or pitcher) Optional: Instead of blue food coloring, use as many servings as necessary of a blue-colored fruit drink or sports drink
- ❏ 1 cup of blueberries (if using the punch bowl or pitcher they could float on top; if using the blender, mix in 10 per person)
- ❏ Optional: vanilla ice cream

Supplies:
- ❏ Clear, tall, plastic cups
- ❏ Blender, punch bowl, or serving pitcher
- ❏ Large spoon
- ❏ Straws or plastic spoons

Directions:
1. For blended drinks combine 1 cup of ice; 1 serving of clear, carbonated soda; a few drops of blue food coloring (or mix in 1 serving of other blue-colored drink); and 10 blueberries in a blender. Blend until all items are thoroughly mixed, about 30 seconds. Pour into a clear glass and serve. Rinse out blender as needed with warm water.
2. For punch bowl or pitcher drinks pour the clear, carbonated soda; a few drops of blue food coloring (or necessary servings of other blue-colored drink); and 1 cup of blueberries (or less depending on the size of your serving dish) to float on top. Optional: Spoon in vanilla ice cream until desired creamy effect is reached and mix it all together with a large spoon. Pour drink into clear, plastic cup. Use a straw or plastic spoon if you want.

PRAYER CHAIN

A SNACKING ACTIVITY THAT CULMINATES IN PRAYER.

BIBLE BASIS:
Matthew 6:9–13

MEMORY VERSE:
"Our Father in heaven, hallowed be your name, your kingdom come, your will be done on earth as it is in heaven. Give us today our daily bread. Forgive us our debts, as we also have forgiven our debtors. And lead us not into temptation, but deliver us from the evil one."
Matthew 6:9–13

BIBLE BACKGROUND

What a blessing that Jesus Christ taught us how to pray! We can learn from Jesus' example here—a lesson on prayer from God Himself.

So how are we to pray? Jesus used the prayer in Matthew 6:9–13 as a model for how to speak to our all-powerful God. We can address God as our Father in heaven. We are to treat God's name in a holy manner. We ask Him to increase the influence of His Kingdom in our lives and times by accomplishing His will (not our personal will) through us here on earth—just as He does through the heavenly hosts all the time in heaven. We can pray for daily needs, including food and necessities. We can forgive and be forgiven, and finally, we can ask for protection from temptation and evil. Jesus prayed this prayer not to say we should pray only in this exact way but to encourage us to offer our praise, worship, and requests to God.

What a privilege to have a lesson on how to pray from the very Son of God, who prayed so passionately while here on earth and now represents us to our Father in heaven (Heb. 7:23–25). Through the Lord's Prayer we recognize God is for us and that He is involved in our lives and provides all we truly need. The students you teach can learn that too.

HINTS FROM THE KITCHEN

🍽️ For this edible project, students munch on corn chips—but they don't just enjoy them with a dip. First, students take either cone-shaped chips or large, rounded chips designed for scooping and place prayer requests inside. Think of this as a corn chip loaded with prayer requests rather than dip.

🍽️ The cone-shaped chips will be a bit more difficult to stuff requests in but the students will enjoy the challenge. The large rounded chips designed for scooping hold the strips of paper easier but only cover the requests. They don't hide requests as the cones do. (Both chips work well for this activity so choose the chip that is most cost-effective for your class size.)

🍽️ Your students will write prayer requests that they share randomly with one other person. Encourage the youth to write heartfelt requests but to remember they will be read by others. If there are requests anyone is uncomfortable sharing with others in the group, invite them to share those requests with you privately and write other requests instead. This activity might offer you a good opportunity to talk about the value and importance of respecting personal information about others and the damage gossip usually causes. Requests should never be repeated to others unless permission has been given by the person making the request. It's also a perfect time to remind students that a prayer request represents a trust in you that should be treasured as a gift and treated with great care. It's a blessing and privilege to pray for each other and be a part of God's incredible work in others' lives.

INGREDIENTS & SUPPLIES
(SERVES 10)

- ❑ 3 bags of cone-shaped corn chips or corn chip scoops (8 chips and an extra handful per student)
- ❑ 2 cups sour cream
- ❑ 1 package of onion or ranch dip seasoning
- ❑ White paper
- ❑ Scissors
- ❑ Pencils or pens
- ❑ Paper plates
- ❑ Plastic spoons
- ❑ Optional: paprika
- ❑ Optional: paper or plastic bowls

CREATIVE COOKERY

***ALLERGY WARNING:** If you have a chef with dairy allergies, offer a dairy-free dip, such as soy-based sour cream, bean dip, or salsa.*

A new twist on chips and dip that inspires prayer!

1. Prior to class, cut white paper into 1" x 4" strips. Each student needs eight strips.

2. Distribute pencils or pens.

3. Have each student write prayer requests on eight strips of paper.

4. Students next place eight cone or scoop-shaped chips on a paper plate.

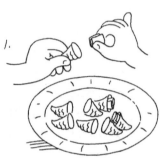

5. Then students insert the prayer requests (hiding the paper as much as possible) inside the corn chips to have eight "prayer-request-dipped" chips on their plates.

6. Have everyone leave their plate of chips as they move about, switching places with other students.

7. At their new plate, each student removes the requests from each chip, reads the requests silently, and keeps them to pray for through the week.

8. Ask students to come forward (either in small groups or individually) to mix more or less of the onion or ranch dip mix into the sour cream according to their tastes. They may use less sour cream if they like, too, for a stronger flavor. Individual or large bowls may be used. (Have students taste using a clean plastic spoon that's then discarded.) Top with paprika if desired.

9. Invite students to put dip on their plates. Pray and enjoy dipped cones or scoops!

SAVOR IT!

Jesus prayed because He knew talking with His Father was essential to their relationship and to accomplishing His Father's will. Jesus taught His disciples (including us) to pray for the same reasons. If Jesus needed to pray, we do too. Prayer is a way to connect to God, to praise Him, and to put our needs and petitions before His throne. Enjoy the access you have to God and take time to pray today.

- **What were some of the things Jesus taught us to pray about?** *(God's will, forgiveness, etc.)*

- **What does the Bible say about when we should pray?** *(The Bible says to pray without ceasing, however, a designated time of prayer can help keep it a consistent part of life.)*

- **What makes it challenging for you to pray sometimes?** *(Students may say feeling tired or falling asleep if they are praying late at night, not knowing what to say, feeling that their requests are too trivial to bother God with, etc.)*

PRAYER CHAIN DIP

A new twist on chips and dip that inspires prayer!

Ingredients:
- ❏ 1 bag of cone-shaped corn chips or chips designed for scooping
- ❏ 1 or 2 cups sour cream
- ❏ 1 package onion or ranch dip mix
- ❏ Optional: paprika (a sprinkling)

Supplies:
- ❏ Plate
- ❏ Bowl
- ❏ Spoon

Directions:
1. Put sour cream in a bowl and mix in 1 package (as little or as much as you like) of onion or ranch dip mix.
2. Mix until smooth.
3. If desired, sprinkle with paprika for color and zest.
4. Open bag of chips, pour on a plate, dip, and enjoy!

FIERY SALSA

GET RID OF THAT TIMID SPIRIT.

BIBLE BASIS:
Mark 5:1–20

MEMORY VERSE:
For God did not give us a spirit of timidity, but a spirit of power, of love and of self-discipline.
2 Timothy 1:7

BIBLE BACKGROUND

The demon-possessed man lived in the region of the Gerasenes, an area on the southwest shore of the Sea of Galilee that was mainly inhabited by Gentiles. Jews considered pigs "unclean" and therefore unfit to eat. It would be very unlikely that Jewish people would have lived in this region known as the Decapolis. This area had cavern tombs that may have served as dwelling places for poor people. This was where Jesus encountered the man who called himself "Legion." The word Legion was a Roman term for a unit of about 6,000 soldiers. The name suggests that the man was possessed by numerous demons.

Fearful of banishment into an eternal abyss (see Luke 8:31), the demons begged Jesus not to send them out of the area. Instead of sending them to the abyss, Jesus sent them into a herd of about 2,000 pigs that rushed down a steep bank into the lake and drowned.

A crowd gathered and came to the tombs to see what had happened. They found the man "sitting there, dressed and in his right mind" (Mark 5:15). Undoubtedly, they had seen the man many times before and knew this was not his usual state. Seeing him sitting there—transformed—frightened them. They may have experienced Jesus' power first hand, but instead of following Him, they rejected Him.

The healed man, however, begged to go with Jesus. Jesus didn't let him, though. Instead, Jesus told him to go home and tell everyone what the Lord had done for him. Jesus not only showed His power in this situation, but also demonstrated His mercy.

HINTS FROM THE KITCHEN

- 🍽 Tell your students to be careful to not get chili powder or juice from the chilies into their eyes, and to be careful not even to touch their eyes. Have students rinse their hands with water after handling the chili powder and green chilies just to be safe.

- 🍽 Since middle school students sometimes encourage one another to take risks, keep an eye and ear out for students who might compete to eat the hottest salsa or engage in other risky behaviors.

- 🍽 There are many ways to get students into small groups. You might form the groups for this recipe according to how hot or mild students like their salsa.

- 🍽 The students will likely give their full attention because of the people involved and the dramatic outcome in this story. Demons and demonic possession, however, might be a frightening subject for some. Reinforce that Jesus is always more powerful than Satan and his demons and that we should not fear because we belong to Jesus and may always call on His name.

INGREDIENTS & SUPPLIES
(SERVES 5)

- ❏ One 14.5 oz. can diced tomatoes
- ❏ One 4 oz. can diced green chilies
- ❏ 1 tablespoon fresh, chopped cilantro
- ❏ 1 teaspoon chili powder
- ❏ 1 bag whole wheat, flour, or corn tortilla chips
- ❏ Can opener
- ❏ Bowls
- ❏ Plastic spoons
- ❏ Paper plates
- ❏ Tablespoon and teaspoon

CREATIVE COOKERY

ALLERGY WARNING: If you have chefs who are allergic to wheat or peanuts, this snack could be dangerous. Corn chips may serve as an alternative, but check first. Also, because this project includes a zesty salsa, be aware of any students with sensitivities to spicy foods.

This salsa has a bit of a kick to it. Add less or more chili powder for a milder or spicier salsa.

1. Form groups of three to five students to make the recipe for themselves. The recipe provided should make enough for five students.

2. Prior to class pour the tomatoes and chilies into separate bowls and provide plastic serving spoons for each bowl.

3. Place chopped cilantro (with tablespoon measure) and chili powder (with teaspoon measure) in bowls.

4. Arrange bag of chips and bowls of ingredients on a table for each group of students.

5. Have each group mix their salsa the way they like it; spicier, with more chili powder, or milder, with less.

6. Have students place chips and salsa on their own paper plates.

7. Say a prayer for the food or invite a volunteer to pray.

8. Dip a chip, and enjoy the concoction!

SAVOR IT!

What a powerful, tongue burning snack! It reminds us of Jesus' incredible power. Jesus used His power in healing the possessed man, but He also showed mercy—both to the man and to the demons. He's the same powerful and merciful God we serve today!

- **Why do you think Jesus interacted with this man when most people would not have come near him?** *(Jesus was showing His compassion and mercy in this instance, He was not afraid of the man, etc.)*

- **What are some ways we see Jesus showing both power and mercy in this Bible passage?** *(He cared for the man, He had power over the demons, He gave the man the ability to tell others about Jesus' power and mercy.)*

- **Share some ways we experience Jesus' power and mercy today.** *(Allow students to freely discuss. Some might share about healings from illness or provision in a time of need.)*

FIERY SALSA

Adjust the spiciness to your own taste—and use it as a "powerful" way to witness to others about Jesus' power. (Just be sure to take any food allergies into account.) Add more chili powder to make it hot, less to keep it mild. Wash your hands after handling the green chilies and chili powder, and be sure to avoid touching or rubbing your eyes as you make this salsa.

RECIPE TO TAKE HOME

Ingredients:
- ❏ One 14.5 oz. can diced tomatoes
- ❏ One 4 oz. can diced green chilies
- ❏ 1 tablespoon fresh, chopped cilantro
- ❏ 1 teaspoon chili powder
- ❏ Whole wheat, flour, or corn tortilla chips

Supplies:
- ❏ Can opener
- ❏ Large bowl
- ❏ Spoon
- ❏ Plate

Directions:
1. Open the can of diced tomatoes and the small can of green chilies. Combine in a large bowl.
2. Mix in the chopped cilantro (1 tablespoon) and chili powder (1 teaspoon). Then stir all ingredients together.
3. Open the bag of chips and serve with the salsa on a plate.
4. Invite someone else to join you. There will be plenty to go around!

FIG-LIKE FAITH

THIS TART FRUIT SALAD WILL PERK UP THE TASTE BUDS.

BIBLE BASIS:
Mark 11:12–14, 20–24

MEMORY VERSE:
This is the confidence we have in approaching God: that if we ask anything according to his will, he hears us.
1 John 5:14

BIBLE BACKGROUND

About six weeks before figs grow on fig trees, tiny leaves appear. During this time, small knobs, although not figs, also grow. If the leaves appear but the knobs do not, it means that fruit is unlikely that particular season. When Jesus saw the fig tree, He was in Jerusalem for the Passover. The particular fig tree Jesus examined had leaves but no knobs. Although it wasn't fig season, Jesus knew this tree would not bear fruit and so He cursed it.

The next day, the disciples saw the tree had withered from its roots. Jesus' words caused a live tree to wither. There are similarities between the fig tree and Jesus' own nation. Neither the fig tree nor Israel were bearing fruit. The religious leaders of Jesus' time were showy (like the leaves) but that was all. They never bore fruit because their teaching was wrong and self-serving, plus they did not show justice, mercy, and faithfulness (Matt. 23). Real fruit never grew in their lives or the lives of those around them.

In Mark 11:24 Jesus said, "Therefore I tell you, whatever you ask for in prayer, believe that you have received it, and it will be yours." God teaches us to pray with confidence, heart-felt conviction, and a pure and contrite heart (v. 25). These are the components that always accompany genuine prayer. God always answers genuine prayer, even if He answers in a way that is different from what we, as humans, want.

Usually Jesus' miracles involved life and health. In this particular circumstance Jesus withered a tree to illustrate genuine prayer, the point of this lesson, but also to show the pending judgment of Israel for its lack of spiritual fruit and response to Messiah.

HINTS FROM THE KITCHEN

- Since many students may be unfamiliar with figs and their taste, this yummy salad will introduce them personally to a key item in the story and help bring the lesson to life.

- Consider having students taste a small piece of fig before making the salad. If they are unfamiliar with the taste of figs, tasting them ahead of time may reassure them that they'll enjoy the salad.

- Apricots or dried plums can be used in place of the figs.

- If allspice is not available, substitute cinnamon or nutmeg.

- Two students might share a salad after dividing it into two plastic bowls.

INGREDIENTS & SUPPLIES
(SERVES 2)

- ❏ 2 small apples, peeled, cored, and diced
- ❏ ¼ teaspoon lemon juice
- ❏ 1 tablespoon apple juice
- ❏ 4 dried or fresh figs, diced
- ❏ Pinch of allspice
- ❏ 2 teaspoons honey
- ❏ Small plastic bowls
- ❏ Large bowls
- ❏ Plastic spoons

CREATIVE COOKERY

Figs are tasty in more than just bar cookies, as this recipe shows.

1. Ahead of time, peel, core, and dice apples into a bowl. Then sprinkle or coat with lemon juice to prevent browning and cover with plastic.

2. In class, form pairs of students who will make a salad to share or divide.

3. Have students place the diced apples in a large plastic bowl.

4. Pour the apple juice over the apples and mix with a plastic spoon.

5. Add in figs.

6. Drizzle 2 teaspoons honey to coat apples and figs.

7. Sprinkle on a dash of allspice.

8. Pray God's blessing on the salad and yourselves prior to eating.

SAVOR IT!

Prayers aren't just something we toss up to God for Him to catch as He pleases. Jesus, in this passage, says that God responds to genuine prayers. Jesus cursed the fig tree; the disciples saw it was withered the next day. Jesus used the withered tree as an object lesson for the purpose of teaching us about prayer. He spoke with conviction on what His Father was doing and God responded. In the same way, when we pray genuinely to God with heart-felt conviction, He answers our prayers.

- How do you feel when God does not answer your prayers in the way you want him to? *(Answers will vary.)*

- Why do you think God doesn't give us answers exactly the way we want them all the time? *(God answers prayer according to His will, not ours. But we can trust that He will always do what is best for us in the end.)*

- Think of a prayer request you have right now. What can we pray together about right now? *(Answers will vary.)*

FIG-LIKE-FAITH FRUIT SALAD

Figs are tasty in more than just bar cookies, as this recipe shows.

Ingredients:
- ❑ 2 small apples, peeled, cored, and diced
- ❑ ¼ teaspoon lemon juice
- ❑ 1 tablespoon apple juice
- ❑ 4 dried or fresh figs, diced (dried apricots or dried plums can be substituted)
- ❑ Pinch of allspice (or pinch of cinnamon or nutmeg)
- ❑ 2 teaspoons honey

Supplies:
- ❑ Large plastic bowl
- ❑ Small plastic bowl
- ❑ Plastic spoon

Directions:
1. Peel, core, and dice two small apples.
2. Mix apples in a bowl with ¼ teaspoon lemon juice to keep apples from turning brown.
3. Add 1 tablespoon apple juice.
4. Mix in figs. Substitute dried apricots or dried plums, if desired.
5. Mix in 2 teaspoons honey and stir the salad until evenly coated.
6. Sprinkle salad with a pinch of allspice (or pinch of cinnamon or nutmeg).
7. Mix all together then pour into a small plastic bowl prior to eating. This healthy fruit salad makes a nice addition to any meal.

POWER BAR

FOCUSING ON CHRIST'S POWER GROWS US INSIDE AND OUT.

BIBLE BASIS:
Luke 5:1–11

MEMORY VERSE:
Be strong in the Lord and in his mighty power.
Ephesians 6:10

BIBLE BACKGROUND

After a night of fishing, Peter probably was ready to quit when Jesus asked him to put out from the shore again. It wasn't easy to wash and stretch the nets, and going out into the water would require redoing all of that work. Regardless of what Peter perceived the outcome to be, he did what Jesus requested of him (Luke 5:5), and the results were miraculous.

It may have seemed coincidental that Jesus was preaching at the same lake where Peter, Andrew, James, and John were fishing. It may appear that He called them as total strangers to leave everything behind and follow Him. However, that likely wasn't the case. These four probably had been familiar with Jesus for a while. It was just at this moment that they were called to leave their fishing behind and follow Jesus.

Leaving everything to follow Jesus isn't always easy. It probably wasn't easy for these fishermen, either. They gave up the comfortable familiarity of life at home and careers that would have spanned their entire lives. What they gained by following Jesus, however, was unmatchable. They realized that following someone with the incredible power of Jesus could only change their lives for the better. Although they suffered on this earth for their faith in Christ, they were transformed by His power and received eternal life. We, too, can have this trade-off. We might not be powerful in the world's eyes, but when we follow Jesus we can be assured that we are experiencing power far greater than the world can ever know!

HINTS FROM THE KITCHEN

- Sunflower seed butter is a peanut butter alternative, often found in grocery stores along with the peanut butter. If your local store doesn't carry it, try a health food store.

- If possible, make more than one batch so students can experiment with different add-ons. If you have multiple groups, each group can share its bars, and unique recipe, with the other groups.

- Provide resealable plastic bags for students who want to take their bars home.

INGREDIENTS & SUPPLIES
(MAKES 16 BARS)

- ❏ 1 cup sunflower seed butter (processed in a nut-free facility)
- ❏ ½ cup honey
- ❏ 3 cups dry, uncooked old-fashioned oatmeal
- ❏ Additional add-ins: colorful candy-coated chocolate pieces, raisins, wheat germ, granola (no nuts), chocolate or carob chips, small pretzel pieces, cereal pieces, etc.
- ❏ Large bowls (1 per group)
- ❏ Large spoons (1 per group)
- ❏ Wax paper
- ❏ Masking tape, 1-inch pieces
- ❏ Permanent markers
- ❏ Wet paper towels or sink (for cleaning hands)
- ❏ Optional: resealable plastic bags

CREATIVE COOKERY

ALLERGY WARNING: Some students could have wheat allergies or gluten intolerance. It's a good idea to ask. Also, for students who have allergies to nuts, avoid granola that has been made in a facility that processes nuts.

1. If desired, divide your large group into small groups, so each group can customize their own recipe. The recipe makes 16 bars.

2. Have each group make a basic power bar recipe combining 1 cup sunflower seed butter, 1/2 cup honey, and 3 cups uncooked old-fashioned oatmeal. Mix together until oatmeal is moistened and begins to be sticky.

3. Have students slowly mix in their choice of add-ins, stirring constantly.

4. Tear or cut sixteen 7"x 5" pieces of wax paper for wrapping bars.

5. Use a spoon to divide the mixture among approximately 16 students. Place each portion on wax paper.

6. Have students shape each of the 16 power bars on the wax paper, then fold the paper around the bar and seal the wax paper with masking tape. Now would be a good time to clean off hands at a sink or with wet paper towels.

7. Let students write a slogan about God's power on the outside of each wrapped bar.

8. Thank God that He is powerful and has provided a power-filled snack for today.

SAVOR IT!

Peter knew Jesus was powerful. If any of his fishermen buddies had suggested going out again, they probably would have gotten the cold shoulder. Peter, however, knew Jesus had the power to do miracles. Since Jesus asked him to fish, Peter was curious enough about the outcome that he set out his nets once again.

- **What happened when Peter trusted God's power and went back out to fish?** *(He saw a miracle; he caught an incredible amount of fish.)*

- **How can we learn to trust Jesus' power more?** *(reading Scripture, praying, watching for evidence of His power, sharing with each other when we see Jesus' power, etc.)*

- **In what areas of your life would you like to see more of Jesus' power?** *(Allow students to freely share. Respond accordingly encouraging their faith, offering to pray together, and so on. If time allows, consider sharing areas in your own life where you've seen Jesus' power as a way to encourage the students' faith.)*

POWER BAR

A great way to start your day or kick-start a sluggish afternoon . . . keep additional bars on hand for whenever you need a power boost!

Ingredients:
- ❑ 1 cup sunflower seed butter (processed in a nut-free facility)
- ❑ ½ cup honey
- ❑ 3 cups dry, uncooked old-fashioned oatmeal
- ❑ Additional add-ins: colorful candy-coated chocolate pieces, raisins, wheat germ, granola, chocolate or carob chips, small pretzel pieces, cereal pieces, etc.

Supplies:
- ❑ Large bowl
- ❑ Large spoon
- ❑ Wax paper
- ❑ Masking tape
- ❑ Permanent marker
- ❑ Resealable plastic bag

Directions:
1. Make a basic power bar mix combining 1 cup sunflower seed butter, ½ cup honey, and 3 cups uncooked old-fashioned oatmeal. Mix together until oatmeal is moistened and begins to be sticky.
2. Stir in your favorite add-ins: colorful candy-coated chocolate pieces, raisins, wheat germ, granola (no nuts), chocolate or carob chips, small pretzel pieces, cereal pieces, etc.
3. Divide the mixture onto 16 pieces of wax paper.
4. Shape each portion into a power bar, then wrap in the wax paper. Seal the wax paper with masking tape.
5. Use a permanent marker to write about God's power on the outside of the wax paper.
6. Store your power bars in a resealable plastic bag.
7. Eat whenever you need a power boost!

HONEY BUTTER

JOHN THE BAPTIST FARE.

BIBLE BASIS:
Luke 7:18–23

MEMORY VERSE:
Believe the miracles,
that you may know
and understand that
the Father is in me,
and I in the Father.
John 10:38b

BIBLE BACKGROUND

Herod Antipas' orders placed John the Baptist in jail. And after a year had passed, John still remained there. John the Baptist's disciples told him about the incredible miracles Jesus was performing. John the Baptist sent two of his disciples to the Lord to ask, "Are you the one who was to come, or should we expect someone else?" (Luke 7:19).

When the men came to Jesus they asked him what John the Baptist requested. At that time, Jesus was curing many people from disease, sicknesses and evil spirits, and giving sight to many who were blind. So Jesus replied to the messengers, "'Go back and report to John what you have seen and heard: The blind receive sight, the lame walk, those who have leprosy are cured, the deaf hear, the dead are raised, and the good news is preached to the poor. Blessed is the man who does not fall away on account of me'" (Luke 7:22–23).

Jesus never rebuked John the Baptist for expressing doubt or misunderstanding. Instead, He went on to say good things about John the Baptist to the crowd. One thing Jesus said was that John the Baptist was not like a reed that bends in whatever direction the wind blows it, but rather was a true prophet. (See Luke 7:24–26.) Deep down John the Baptist knew who Jesus was, for he had been Jesus' messenger. Jesus' miracles, however, reaffirmed to him that Jesus was indeed the promised Messiah.

In weak moments, some Christians may doubt, but the life-changing truth of who Jesus is can erase that doubt. We need look no further than Jesus for the answers.

HINTS FROM THE KITCHEN

- Today's lesson about doubt may be difficult for some in your group. When it comes to salvation through Jesus Christ a leap of faith is necessary. Even as believers some young people may worry that having doubts indicates they don't have faith. People may have doubts about matters of faith. This lesson reassures students that they can always ask questions and express issues of concern related to their faith. Questioning is not necessarily the same as rejecting Jesus. Sincere Christians may have questions related to their faith. That is what our earthly spiritual journey is all about.

- As students taste today's snack, use it as an opportunity to bring biblical people and their culture to life. Remind students that Scripture mentions that John the Baptist regularly ate honey (Matt. 3:4), and that the bread of his time was often something similar to what we call pita bread today.

INGREDIENTS & SUPPLIES
(SERVES 10)

- ❏ 8 tablespoons soft margarine spread
- ❏ 8 tablespoons applesauce
- ❏ 4 tablespoons honey
- ❏ Bread, crackers, or pita bread
- ❏ Tablespoon
- ❏ Teaspoon
- ❏ Plastic bowls
- ❏ Plastic spoons and knives
- ❏ Optional: 4 tablespoons vanilla yogurt

CREATIVE COOKERY

*ALLERGY WARNING: *This honey butter will be served with bread so be aware of wheat allergies among the students in your group. If dairy allergies are an issue, simply drizzle the bread with honey.*

John the Baptist ate locusts and honey, but this honey butter will be much tastier—guaranteed!

1. Have students measure and mix eight tablespoons of soft margarine spread, eight tablespoons of applesauce, four tablespoons of honey and the optional four tablespoons of vanilla yogurt (if including that) in a plastic bowl. Stir together until creamy using a plastic spoon.

2. Have students choose either bread, crackers, or pita bread to go with their honey butter.

3. Pray or have a volunteer pray to ask God's blessing on the food.

4. With a plastic knife, spread honey butter on the bread, crackers, or pita bread. Enjoy!

SAVOR IT!

John the Baptist spent much of his adult life proclaiming the Messiah. It may seem odd that he questioned whether Jesus was this Messiah. But the questions are more understandable when you consider that John the Baptist was in a jail cell. Yet John the Baptist knew enough from the Old Testament Scriptures that Jesus' teaching and miracles confirmed that He was indeed the Messiah. John the Baptist was reassured. Jesus understands the challenges we face. He can help us when we feel doubts about our faith. Look to Jesus and see His work on the cross and His resurrection. Believe that Jesus is who He says He is!

- **What things in your life make it easy to doubt?** (*sickness, death, trouble at home, problems at school, world events, etc.*)

- **What should you do when doubts creep in?** (*Study your Bible to understand its message and truth, ask God to show you Himself through His Word, pray to God and ask for greater faith, talk to a strong Christian and have him or her help answer questions you may have, etc.*)

- **How can focusing on Jesus help us with doubt?** (*When we take our doubts to God and let Him reassure us and guide our lives, we find He addresses those doubts through His Word and in other ways. And as we get to know Jesus better, we can find comfort in who He is, even as we face our doubts together with Him.*)

HONEY BUTTER

John the Baptist ate locusts and honey but this honey butter will be much tastier—guaranteed!

Ingredients:
- ❏ 4 tablespoons soft margarine spread
- ❏ 4 tablespoons applesauce
- ❏ 2 tablespoons honey
- ❏ Bread, crackers, or pita bread
- ❏ Optional: 2 tablespoons vanilla yogurt

Supplies:
- ❏ Tablespoon
- ❏ Teaspoon
- ❏ Plastic bowl
- ❏ Plastic spoon
- ❏ Plastic knife

Directions:
1. Use a measuring spoon to measure 4 tablespoons of butter, 4 tablespoons of applesauce, 2 tablespoons of honey and (if you want) the optional 2 tablespoons of vanilla yogurt in a plastic bowl. Use a plastic spoon to stir together until creamy.
2. With a plastic knife, spread honey butter on the bread, crackers, or pita bread. Enjoy.

PERSONIFIED PARFAITS

BIBLE BASIS:
John 1:1–18

MEMORY VERSE:
No one has ever seen God, but God the One and Only, who is at the Father's side, has made him known.
John 1:18

BIBLE BACKGROUND

The Gospel of John begins with the same words as Genesis, "In the beginning . . ." John records that the Word (Jesus) existed in the beginning. This reality challenges our comprehension. We can barely even grasp when the beginning was, since it was way before our time. Yet Jesus existed—was with God—then.

John's Gospel also states that the Word (Jesus) wasn't just with God, He *was* God. So when Jesus came to earth as a baby, God became human. We can't fully understand such a miracle, but Jesus became human while still remaining God in order to make God known to us (John 1:18).

John 1:7 introduces us to a witness for Jesus. This witness was John the Baptist, Jesus' cousin. When John was still a baby in his mother's womb he leapt for joy when Jesus was near. In John 1:29–34 John the Baptist baptized Jesus and announced Jesus' purpose for coming: to take away the sins of the world.

In John 1:12–13 we learn that all who believe in Jesus, or receive Him, become children of God. To be "born of God" (vs. 13) is what we call today being "born again" or "being born of the spirit." This is possible because Jesus came to earth as a helpless baby. He left the majesty of heaven to come and be born to earthly parents. Jesus was distinctly different from all humans because He was without sin. He was fully God, yet he was still human at the same time. Such a thing we can't comprehend; we can only thank Him for becoming human!

HINTS FROM THE KITCHEN

- The marshmallow faces allow a creative opportunity for your students. Let them have fun.

- To reduce costs, create the marshmallow faces out of ingredients you already purchased for the parfaits such as cranberry eyes, strawberry mouth, and a granola piece nose. Additional ideas include chocolate chips and sprinkles.

- For easy serving, set up a table with all the ingredients placed in disposable bowls with plastic spoons. The whipped cream may be kept in its own can or plastic container.

INGREDIENTS & SUPPLIES
(SERVES 10)

- ❏ Clear, tall plastic cups (1 per student)
- ❏ Five 1-cup tubs flavored yogurt (strawberry, vanilla, blueberry, raspberry, etc.)
- ❏ 5 cups granola cereal or crushed granola bars
- ❏ 5 cups fruit such as strawberries, peaches, or blueberries
- ❏ 1 can whipped cream
- ❏ 1 package large marshmallows
- ❏ Marshmallow "face" ingredients (see Hints from the Kitchen)

CREATIVE COOKERY

ALLERGY WARNING: *If you have students with nut allergies, obtain granola cereal or bars without nuts that were not processed on equipment used to process nuts. Some students could be allergic to strawberries or other berries as well. Choose other fruits such as peaches for substitutes. If dairy allergies are a concern, replace the yogurt with either a soy-based yogurt or a dairy-free sorbet.*

These colorful and healthy parfaits would be a decorative addition to any party table.

1. Have each student spoon parfait ingredients into a plastic cup, layering in this order: yogurt, granola pieces, and fruit. Repeat until parfait is colorfully layered and the cup is full.

2. Top with whipped cream.

3. Make a marshmallow face by inserting chocolate chips, candy sprinkles, cranberries, strawberry pieces, and larger granola pieces into a marshmallow. Position the marshmallow face on top of the whipped cream. Encourage creativity as students make their faces.

4. Say a prayer or invite a volunteer to ask God to bless the food.

SAVOR IT!

Because we're human, it's hard to imagine what it means to be something greater, to be God. But when we meet Jesus, we meet God. You made each of your parfaits personal and unique. Because Jesus was both human *and* God when he was here on earth, he can understand each of us in a personal and unique way. What an amazing Savior—one who is all-powerful God, but who also understands and loves each one of us personally.

- Why do you think Jesus was willing to become human for us? *(He loved us, He knew it was the only way for us to become reconciled to God, He was obedient to God's plan, He knew only a sinless God could redeem a sinful people, etc.)*

- What's one way you can show Jesus how thankful you are that He became human on your behalf? *(pray and thank Him, follow Him, tell others about Him, live in His will, etc.)*

- What is appealing to us, as humans, about Jesus becoming human? *(We know Jesus understands what we go through; He experienced all that we experience, yet He did it without sin.)*

PERSONIFIED PARFAITS

RECIPE TO TAKE HOME

Grab a few friends and make these healthy and colorful parfaits. The more colors you can add by way of flavored yogurt and fruit toppings, the better your parfait will look. As you personalize your parfaits, share about the Savior, Jesus, who understands each one of us in a personal and unique way.

Ingredients:
- ❑ 1 cup flavored yogurt (strawberry, vanilla, blueberry, raspberry, etc.)
- ❑ 1 cup granola cereal or crushed granola bars
- ❑ 1 cup fruit, such as strawberries, peaches, or blueberries
- ❑ 1 can whipped cream
- ❑ Large marshmallows
- ❑ Your selection of chocolate chips, sprinkles, cranberries, strawberry pieces, and granola pieces

Supplies:
- ❑ Clear, tall plastic cup
- ❑ Plastic bowls and plastic spoons for serving the ingredients

Directions:
1. Take a clear, tall plastic cup and begin spooning in the parfait ingredients.
2. Layer your parfait with yogurt, granola pieces, and fruit. Repeat until parfait is colorfully layered and the cup is full.
3. Top with whipped cream and a marshmallow face you make on a large marshmallow with chocolate chips, sprinkles, and other items.
4. Use a plastic spoon to eat your parfait creation. Yum!

EYE-POPPIN' DIP

TANGY WEENIES MAKE FOR A DIP-ROARING TIME.

BIBLE BASIS:
John 1:35–45

MEMORY VERSE:
I will tell of the kindnesses of the LORD, the deeds for which he is to be praised.
Isaiah 63:7a

BIBLE BACKGROUND

After spending a day with Jesus, Andrew became convinced that Jesus was in fact the real Messiah, or Christ (John 1:35–39).

Andrew shared this discovery with Simon Peter while Philip told Nathanael. Soon the word spread across the countryside and multitudes of people came to Jesus. Jesus' ministry expanded through word of mouth, much as it does today.

One reason Jesus' ministry spread so quickly was because of John the Baptist's work, which prepared Jesus' way. John's witness that Jesus was the Lamb of God was key to the events in John 1:35–45. The disciples followed Jesus at that point in large part because John identified Him.

John called Jesus the "Lamb of God," which showed he understood Jesus to be the one who would take away the people's sin (John 1:29). John told two of his disciples who Jesus was and convinced them to follow Jesus. John 1:40–41 tells us that Andrew was one of these two disciples. Although the two disciples originally called Jesus, "Rabbi," meaning teacher, Andrew eventually called Jesus Messiah, showing that he understood who Jesus truly was.

As you share Scripture with young teens, you introduce them to Jesus. That seems a simple outreach, but it's profound. The teens you reach have probably already seen a difference in your life. If so, all you have to do is explain why you're different—because you've met Jesus and live in the hope He gives.

HINTS FROM THE KITCHEN

- Little weenies are sold in the refrigerated or frozen meat sections of most grocery stores.

- If you heat the weenies at home, take them warm in the slow cooker and turn the slow cooker to low when you arrive, keeping the weenies warm for your students.

INGREDIENTS & SUPPLIES
(SERVES 10)

- ❏ 2 pkgs. pre-cooked weenies (mini hot dogs)
- ❏ 1 cup water
- ❏ Two 12-ounce jars honey
- ❏ Two 18-ounce bottles barbeque sauce
- ❏ Two 12-ounce bottles chili sauce
- ❏ 1 or 2 shakes of paprika
- ❏ Sprinkle of parsley flakes
- ❏ Slow cooker
- ❏ Paper towel
- ❏ Large bowl
- ❏ Large spoon
- ❏ Toothpicks
- ❏ Paper or plastic plates

CREATIVE COOKERY

Nothing like eye-poppin' dip to get the taste buds going. Don't expect this snack to last long! Toothpicks add up to even more fun.

1. Ahead of time, heat weenies in a slow cooker with 1 cup water.

2. Students use a spoon to mix dip in a large bowl using all the ingredients listed (except the weenies and water).

3. Drain weenies on a paper plate with a paper towel on it. Remove the paper towel and put weenies on a serving plate. Have students put some dip on their paper or plastic plates (not share it out of the large dip bowl) and use toothpicks to place a few weenies on their plates as well.

4. Say a prayer or invite a volunteer to ask God's blessing on the food. Dig in. (There probably won't be leftovers and may not even be seconds—a sure hit!)

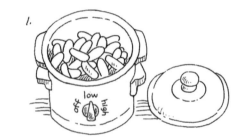

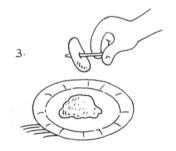

SAVOR IT!

We all experience eye-opening moments.
Following Jesus Christ and living as His disciple is the most eye-opening experience a person can have in this world. Help others open their eyes to Jesus as well by boldly sharing with them about His love and plan for them!

- **What have been some eye-opening experiences in your life?** *(Answers will vary.)*

- **How did John the Baptist open the eyes of the two disciples mentioned in today's lesson?** *(John proclaimed the Messiah's coming, and when the Messiah had come John directed people to Him so they could follow Him.)*

- **How has Jesus opened your eyes to the world?** *(He has helped me see my sin, made me more aware of sin around me, given me a heart for unsaved people, etc.)*

- **How can you help your friends meet Jesus and open their eyes to who He is?** *(by talking about what I believe, by bringing them to church, by answering their questions, by living as God commands, etc.)*

RECIPE TO TAKE HOME

EYE-POPPIN' DIP

People coming over to play a game or do homework? Tired of chips? Try some eye-poppin' dip and weenies on toothpicks. A sure winner every time!

Ingredients:
- ❏ One 6-oz. serving package of pre-cooked weenies (mini hot dogs)
- ❏ 1/2 cup water
- ❏ One 12-ounce jar honey
- ❏ One 18-ounce bottle barbeque sauce
- ❏ One 12-ounce bottle chili sauce
- ❏ Paprika
- ❏ Parsley flakes

Supplies:
- ❏ Slow cooker
- ❏ Bowl for sauce
- ❏ Large spoon
- ❏ Paper plates
- ❏ Toothpicks

Directions:

1. Heat weenies and ½ cup water in a slow cooker on low for one hour. Try to not open the lid of the slow cooker while heating.

2. Use a large spoon to mix dip ingredients together in a bowl: honey, barbeque sauce, chili sauce, and paprika. Sprinkle with parley flakes.

3. When weenies are heated through, drain on a paper towel on a plate. Remove and throw away the paper towel. Use toothpicks to transfer the weenies to your own plate and add some eye-poppin' dip on the side.

FROZEN COOKIE DELIGHTS

ADD NEW LIFE TO YOUR COOKIE WITH A FROZEN TREAT BETWEEN.

BIBLE BASIS:
John 3:1–8, 16–21, 36

MEMORY VERSE:
"I tell you the truth, no one can see the kingdom of God unless he is born again."
John 3:3

BIBLE BACKGROUND

Nicodemus was a Pharisee. Jesus called him "Israel's teacher," which may mean Nicodemus was the head of a rabbinic school.

One night, Nicodemus approached Jesus and said, "Rabbi, we know you are a teacher who has come from God. For no one could perform the miraculous signs you are doing if God were not with him" (John 3:2). Jesus replied, "I tell you the truth, no one can see the kingdom of God unless he is born again" (John 3:3).

These words confused Nicodemus, so he asked, "How can a man be born when he is old? . . . Surely he cannot enter a second time into his mother's womb to be born!" (John 3:4).

Jesus explained that being born again is a spiritual rather than physical thing. He then gently chastised Nicodemus for being a teacher of the law yet not understanding these things. Jesus said, "I have spoken to you of earthly things and you do not believe; how then will you believe if I speak of heavenly things?" (John 3:12).

We can't earn salvation by going to church or by doing good works. It's a gift from God (Eph. 2:8–9), given freely. We simply need to trust Christ for it. Reflect today on the new life Jesus offers.

HINTS FROM THE KITCHEN

- Today's edible project includes cookies, either store-bought or homemade. Large graham crackers can also be used.

- To keep the ice cream from melting, transport it in a cooler filled with ice and, if possible, place ice cream in a freezer prior to your group time.

- Freezing the cookies first, and making the treats while they are cold, keeps the sandwiches from breaking and falling apart.

- Today's lesson gives you a great opportunity to give some context to the famous verse, John 3:16. By understanding the story of Nicodemus, your students will appreciate it all the more and realize God's great love for them.

INGREDIENTS & SUPPLIES

- ❏ Large, unfrosted, homemade or store-bought cookies (2 per student)
- ❏ ½ gal. store-bought ice cream (any flavor)
- ❏ Paper plates
- ❏ Ice cream scoop

CREATIVE COOKERY

ALLERGY WARNING: *For this treat, be aware of wheat allergies or dairy intolerances in your group.*

A quick and easy way to spruce up a simple snack! These ice cream sandwiches are simply delightful.

1. Take one large cookie and place it on your paper plate with the bottom, flat side facing up.

2. Scoop a small portion of ice cream and place it on the cookie. Spread just enough ice cream to cover most of the cookie or the ice cream will ooze out.

3. Place the second cookie on top of the ice cream—bottom, flat side facing down.

4. Grab both cookies and gently press together, taking care not to break the cookies.

5. Pray and eat quickly before it melts!

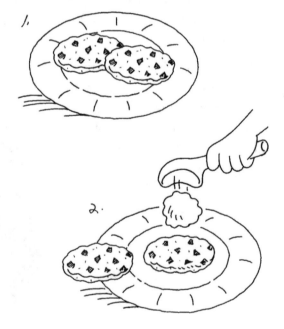

SAVOR IT!

Jesus took the time to teach Nicodemus what it means to be born again. Although Jesus often rebuked Pharisees, He knew that was not what Nicodemus needed. The fact that Nicodemus came to Jesus at night could symbolize his sincere desire to know what it means to have new life. God loved us so much He sent Jesus. Jesus offers new life to anyone who believes in Him. That's something God wants us all to understand. Consider using ice cream to bring some new life to your cookies at home. It will be a great opportunity to share about new life in Jesus with a friend.

- **What does it mean to be born again?** (*being born again means a renewed spiritual birth, accepting Jesus into your heart, having God transform your life and renew you, etc.*)

- **What are some things people today think will bring them new life, spiritually?** (*being good, learning about various religions, following false religions, thinking positive thoughts, etc.*)

- **How would you explain being born again to a non-Christian?** (*Being born again comes from believing in Jesus and having Him in your life.*)

FROZEN COOKIE DELIGHTS

Bring new life to plain cookies with a bit of ice cream. Eat these quickly before they melt! After seeing how easy these are to make you might never have plain ice cream again.

Ingredients:
- ❑ 2 large, unfrosted, homemade or store-bought cookies (Graham crackers will also work.)
- ❑ Store-bought ice cream (any flavor)

Supplies:
- ❑ Paper plate
- ❑ Ice cream scoop
- ❑ Optional: plastic wrap

Directions:
1. Take one large cookie and place it on your paper plate with the bottom, flat side facing up.
2. Scoop a small portion of ice cream and place it on the cookie. Put only enough ice cream to cover up most of the cookie or the ice cream will ooze out.
3. Take the second cookie and place it on top of the ice cream, flat side facing down.
4. Grab both cookies and gently press together, taking care not to break the cookies.
5. If you'd like, freeze a couple of these for later. Wrap snuggly in plastic wrap, then place in the freezer.

SALAD SHAKERS

SHAKE THINGS UP A BIT WITH A SALAD GRAB BAG.

BIBLE BASIS:
John 5:39–46

MEMORY VERSE:
But these are written
that you may believe
that Jesus is the Christ,
the Son of God,
and that by believing
you may have life
in his name.
John 20:31

BIBLE BACKGROUND

When Jesus broke Sabbath tradition and also claimed to be God's Son, many Jewish religious leaders grew angry and sought to kill Him. Jesus' response to their accusations was simple: Believe and follow the instructions you so diligently study! If you believe Moses, then you should believe what he said about the promised Messiah (Jesus). (See Gen. 3:15; 49:10; Deut. 18:15–19.)

These men studied the Scriptures hoping to find eternal life (John 5:39–40), but they didn't believe that these Scriptures referred to Jesus. Although these men were eager to accept the praise of men and of each other, they couldn't accept God's truth—even though He was right in front of them. Jesus didn't point fingers at these men. He said that He wouldn't accuse them before His Father God. He wouldn't need to. They stood condemned already by Moses, on whom they set their hopes. Jesus concludes by saying, "If you believed Moses, you would believe me, for he wrote about me" (John 5:46).

In today's world, Christian middle school students need to stand firm in their faith. It's not popular to say there's only one way to God. Some would say that's not being tolerant. Yet, the Bible teaches this truth. Just as Jesus' words were not popular with the Jewish religious leaders, your students' words of truth also may be unpopular. Teach your students to accept God's message and tell others the message of truth with conviction. It won't be an easy way, but it *is* God's way.

HINTS FROM THE KITCHEN

- For today's edible project students will make salad shakers. To tie in to today's lesson focus, mention that as Christians we are often shaken by those who disagree with us. We try to proclaim truth, but we are criticized or called intolerant, narrow minded, and unscientific. It may be hard to hear these things, but Christians can't let what the world thinks of them affect them. We can be shaken but ultimately we must stand firm in our faith.

- Thoroughly shake these salads for the best possible taste.

- For easy assembly, set up all ingredients on a table where students can easily access items. Place all salad fillers in individual plastic bowls with a plastic fork for serving. Clearly display various dressings (in the bottle is fine).

INGREDIENTS & SUPPLIES
(FOR UP TO 6)

- ❏ Zippered, quart-size plastic bags
- ❏ 1 bag assorted salad greens including your selection of romaine, iceberg, spinach, and baby greens
- ❏ Salad fillers including your choice of cherry tomatoes or diced tomatoes, black olives, shaved carrots, raisins, cranberry raisins, cheese cubes, diced ham or turkey, cut up radishes, diced cucumbers, mandarin oranges, chopped celery, croutons, or other items
- ❏ Salad dressings including your choice of regular and low-fat French, Italian, Caesar, Thousand Island, Ranch, Raspberry Vinaigrette, and Asian
- ❏ Plastic bowls
- ❏ Plastic forks

CREATIVE COOKERY

A fun-filled salad is just what's needed! Try a new topping while you have the chance, or a dressing you wouldn't normally have. Shake things up! Why not?

1. Have students make their individual salads in small groups of three or four. Invite them to fill a zippered plastic bag with whatever salad greens and fillers they choose. When they are finished, have them top it with their favorite dressing.

2. Have students zip their bags closed, then shake their salads until all ingredients are evenly covered with salad dressing.

3. Allow students to eat their salads right out of the bag with a fork!

4. As you thank God for the food, thank Him also that He holds on to us when we are shaken.

SAVOR IT!

Jesus is God's message for us to accept. John 20:31 says, "But these are written that you may believe that Jesus is the Christ, the Son of God, and that by believing you may have life in his name." **As Christians we need to stand firm on our foundation—and our faith in the truth of God's message—no matter what the world throws our way!**

- **What does it mean to be a Christian?** *(follow Christ, believe Jesus died to forgive me of my sins, etc.)*

- **In today's society where it isn't popular to say there is only one way to heaven, what are you as a Christian to do?** *(No matter how difficult, I can't compromise the message. I must stay true to the words of the Bible, popular or not.)*

- **How can sharing your faith with others benefit them?** *(Everyone needs Jesus. By sharing God's truth with others, you can help them know Jesus so ultimately they find faith in Him for their salvation.)*

- **Why do you think it's difficult for people to accept Jesus' message?** *(People don't want to hear that there's only one way to heaven, people don't want to give up their sin, etc.)*

SALAD SHAKERS

Next time it's your turn to help with dinner, shake things up with these salad shakers in a bag. Added plus: no dirty dishes!

Ingredients:
- ❏ Salad greens such as romaine, iceberg, spinach, etc.
- ❏ Salad fillers: cherry tomatoes or diced tomatoes, black olives, shaved carrots, raisins, cranberry raisins, cheese cubes, diced ham or turkey, cut up radishes, diced cucumber, mandarin oranges, chopped celery, croutons, or other items
- ❏ Salad dressings such as regular or low-fat French, Italian, Caesar, Thousand Island, Ranch, Raspberry Vinaigrette, and Asian

Supplies:
- ❏ Zippered, quart-size plastic bags
- ❏ Plastic bowls
- ❏ Plastic forks

Directions:
1. Place all salad fillers in individual plastic bowls with a plastic fork for serving.
2. Display various dressings in the bottles.
3. Take a zippered plastic bag and fill it with whatever salad fillers you and your family or friends choose. When finished, top salad with a favorite dressing.
4. Shake the salad in the zipped bag to move ingredients around and cover everything evenly with salad dressing.
5. Eat with a plastic fork right out of the bag.

HEALTHY BOOST

BLENDED WITH HEALTHY FRUITS ... WHO NEEDS PROTEIN POWDER?

BIBLE BASIS:
John 14:15–21, 26

MEMORY VERSE:
So I say, live by the Spirit, and you will not gratify the desires of the sinful nature.
Galatians 5:16

BIBLE BACKGROUND

Christians can't earn salvation, and they can't earn the Holy Spirit either. Rather, God sends the Holy Spirit to live in our hearts to teach, convict, guide, comfort, and intercede on our behalf (John 14:15–16; 16:8–11, 13; Rom. 8:14–16, 26–27). As we obey Christ, the Holy Spirit helps us to grow. Think of the Holy Spirit as the best teacher available!

Jesus is "God with us," and, if we are believers, the Holy Spirit is "God within us" (John 14:17). Paul described the life and fruit of the Holy Spirit in Galatians 5:16–26. The gifts of the Spirit are listed in Romans 12:6–8, 1 Corinthians 12—14; and Ephesians 4:7, 11–13. Check out these passages to see what those gifts are. The Holy Spirit helps us and works in our daily lives. When you feel guilt about sin or a prodding to speak to someone about spiritual things, these are most likely the working of the Holy Spirit within you.

In addition, the Holy Spirit reminds us of things Jesus said. The Holy Spirit also acts as a counselor, a spirit of truth (John 14:16–17). Jesus promised that the Holy Spirit would be God's gift to believers (John 14:16, 26). As mysterious as the work of the Holy Spirit is, the results of His work are very evident in the everyday life of an individual believer, as well as in the Body of Christ.

HINTS FROM THE KITCHEN

- For this project, students make a healthy smoothie. Suggested ingredients are given but feel free to add additional ingredients that you think your students will enjoy.

- To tie this project into the lesson, ask students if they have ever had a healthy power drink and what types of drinks they like to order. Ask if they ever put additional "boosts" into their drinks such as protein powder, immunity boost, or vitamins. Explain that the Holy Spirit's role in our lives is similar to a healthy power drink in that He strengthens us and keeps us spiritually healthy. He also provides "boosts" in our prayer life, our Bible understanding, and our ability to witness to others.

- Smoothies usually come out smoother when made in a blender so this is the recommended option. However, a blender is not required and your students may have more fun stirring, smooshing, and smashing fruit. Be sure to dice and slice the fruit ahead of time.

- When making different flavors of blended drinks, rinse the blender with water between each recipe to avoid mixing flavors.

INGREDIENTS & SUPPLIES

- ❏ Fruit and juices for blending: bananas, peaches, strawberries, orange juice, pineapple juice, mango juice, blueberries, pears, kiwi, and orange slices (1 cup total fruit per student)
- ❏ Other drink additions: milk, yogurt, ice cream, and wheat germ (½ cup total per student)
- ❏ Blender
- ❏ Tall, clear cups
- ❏ Straws
- ❏ Spoons

CREATIVE COOKERY

*ALLERGY WARNING: *Watch out for potential allergy concerns as you choose your ingredients. Strawberries may be an issue for some children. Wheat and dairy products may also be a concern when using milk, yogurt, ice cream, or wheat germ.*

Everyone can use a boost. Give this drink a try and enjoy the extra energy.

1. Before class, peel all fruit such as bananas.

2. If a blender is available, display drink options on a table near the counter where the blender is plugged in. Invite students to choose one or two ingredients for their drink and have them (or help them) "blend" away. For creamier drinks, have students add milk, yogurt, or ice cream.

3. For fruit-based drinks, have students choose orange juice, pineapple juice, or mango juice.

4. If no blender is available, have students mix their own drinks in a pitcher using a long, strong spoon. Fruits will need to be diced and sliced ahead of time.

5. Pour individual drinks into the tall, clear cups from either the pitcher or the blender. Give students straws and spoons if desired. Have students explain what's in their drink to at least one other person and share what they like best about it.

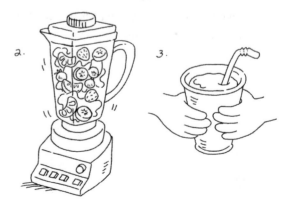

SAVOR IT!

The Holy Spirit's jobs include many things. Since the Holy Spirit is a helper, a teacher, and God Himself, there's no need to be afraid to hear what He says or to do what He asks. Sometimes we get so busy and self-sufficient that we don't listen for the Holy Spirit's prodding. Staying aware of the Holy Spirit's work in our lives is very important. As we become tuned-in to Him, we will be able to do as He prompts.

- **What kinds of things might the Holy Spirit help you do?** *(witness to someone, resist sin, read the Bible, pray, ask for forgiveness, etc.)*

- **Share about some times when the Holy Spirit worked in your life or in the life of someone you know.** *(Allow students to freely share, and consider sharing a time from your own life.)*

- **Why do you think Christians sometimes forget about the Holy Spirit working in them?** *(It's easy to think that we're doing things by ourselves. In reality, we're helpless without the Holy Spirit's intervention.)*

HEALTHY BOOST

Need a boost? Want to give one to someone else? Mix in some fruity ingredients and blend away. Surprise a friend or family member with this healthy, refreshing drink.

Ingredients:

❑ Fruit and juice for blending: bananas, peaches, strawberries, orange juice, pineapple juice, mango juice, blueberries, pears, kiwis, and orange slices (Fruit ingredients will need to be diced and sliced if a blender is not used)

❑ Additional add-ins: milk, yogurt or ice cream, and wheat germ

Supplies:

❑ Blender
❑ Tall, clear cups
❑ Straws
❑ Spoons

Directions:

1. If a blender is available, choose two or three ingredients for your drink and "blend" away. For creamier drinks, add milk, yogurt, or ice cream. For fruit-based drinks, choose orange juice, pineapple juice, or mango juice. If no blender is available, mix your own drink in a pitcher using a long, strong spoon. Ingredients such as fruits will need to be diced and sliced ahead of time.

2. Pour into a tall, clear cup from either the pitcher or the blender. Sip your fruity concoction for a special boost.

HEARTFELT LOVE DIP

START WITH A GREAT FONDUE THAT SAYS, "I'M FOND OF YOU."

BIBLE BASIS:
1 Corinthians 13

MEMORY VERSE:
Love is patient,
love is kind.
It does not envy,
it does not boast,
it is not proud.
1 Corinthians 13:4

BIBLE BACKGROUND

Love is something everyone needs and most everyone wants to give. The love described in 1 Corinthians 13 is a godly love. This kind of love isn't often seen in the world. It's a love that looks out for others and puts them first. In other parts of the first letter from Paul to the Corinthians, he discussed their lack of love for one another. Now in Chapter 13, Paul describes what real love is like.

Paul states that there are many important things in life but the greatest of them is love. Without love, the results or manifestations of our gifts of prophecy, tongues, and faith mean nothing.

Godly love is shown by being patient and kind, not being envious, not boasting or being proud, not being rude or self-seeking, not getting easily angered or holding a grudge, and not delighting in evil. It's rejoicing in the truth, protecting and taking care of others, trusting others, believing in others, and having hope.

Sometimes we say "I love ..." too easily. We apply it to our pets, our friends, our family members, our favorite restaurant, chocolate, and even fast food. Can we really equate all of these things on the same level? Try a little experiment. Instead of saying love all of the time, try to say it only when you really mean it. And show it. Tell a parent or a friend, and then show your love to them by following through with a kind deed. Switch all other uses of the term love to words such as *like, appreciate, value, or enjoy.* See if it makes you appreciate *love* more. If nothing else, at least the exercise might clarify love. Regardless, remember that our human love pales in comparison to God's love for us. John 15:13 states, "Greater love has no one than this, that he lay down his life for his friends." Jesus laid down His life for us. He calls us friends. Walk in His love as you share your love with others.

HINTS FROM THE KITCHEN

- Most items used in this lesson are finger foods but for those that are not, use skewers or toothpicks.

- You may provide just one dipping item, such as apples, or offer all the food choices if your budget allows.

- Be sure to peel, cut, and remove stems ahead of time. Remove any wrappers too.

- This recipe provides for 12 to 16 students but can be easily cut in half for smaller groups.

INGREDIENTS & SUPPLIES
(SERVES 12-16)

- ❏ 1 cup caramel ice cream topping
- ❏ Two 8 oz. tubs whipped cream
- ❏ Dipping items: apples, bananas, marshmallows, chocolate bars, graham crackers, strawberries, and pineapple chunks (fresh or canned)
- ❏ Can opener (if necessary, for canned fruit)
- ❏ Small paper or plastic bowls
- ❏ Plastic spoons
- ❏ Disposable wooden bamboo skewers, reusable metal skewers, or toothpicks

CREATIVE COOKERY

ALLERGY WARNING: Watch out for potential allergy concerns as you choose your ingredients. Strawberries may be an issue for some students. Wheat may also be a concern when using graham crackers.

This heartfelt love dip is a sure-fire way to show someone your sweet side and to spread some love around.

1. Prior to class, unwrap dipping items, remove peels, and discard stems. Then serve the treats in individual paper or plastic bowls. Place these dishes of dipping items on a table for students' easy access. Place napkins and toothpicks or skewers on the table.

2. Have volunteers help you mix ½ cup of caramel sauce into each tub of whipped cream. Add these to your table.

3. Pray or have a volunteer pray and bless the food.

4. Invite students to come to the table in small groups of three or four. Students help themselves to fill a small bowl with their servings of sweet dip and dipping items. Make skewers or toothpicks available, if necessary.

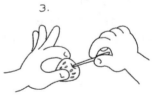

5. When all students have had a serving invite them to return for seconds.

SAVOR IT!

Loving people who love us isn't difficult, but loving those who are unloving to us sometimes is. It's okay to step out of your comfort zone a little and reach out to those around you in thoughtful and caring ways.

- **How do you show love to those around you?** *(by obeying parents, by helping my younger sister with her homework, doing yard work for a neighbor, being a part of a charity or help organization, etc.)*

- **What parts of love mentioned in 1 Corinthians 13 are most difficult for you?** *(Let your students share openly.)*

- **How does God show the love mentioned in 1 Corinthians 13?** *(He is patient as we grow, He forgives our sins, He is never rude, He sacrificed Himself, etc.)*

HEARTFELT LOVE DIP

This heartfelt love dip is a sure-fire way to show someone your sweet side and to spread some love around.

Ingredients:
- ❏ ½ cup caramel sauce (ice cream topping)
- ❏ One 8 oz. tub whipped cream (serves 6–8)
- ❏ Dipping items: apples, bananas, marshmallows, chocolate bars, graham crackers, strawberries, and pineapple chunks (fresh or canned)

Supplies:
- ❏ Can opener (if necessary, for canned fruit)
- ❏ Small paper or plastic bowls
- ❏ Plastic spoons
- ❏ Disposable wooden bamboo skewers, reusable metal skewers, or toothpicks

Directions:
1. Unwrap dipping items, remove peels and stems, and serve in individual paper or plastic bowls.
2. Mix ½ cup of caramel sauce into the whipped cream tub. Spoon your own serving of sweet dip into a bowl for dipping items. Refrigerate the rest of the dip. (Don't dip items directly into this dip unless you intend to eat most of it. Discard any leftovers.)
3. Use skewers or toothpicks for dipping items if needed.

PROMISE CROSSES

A REFLECTION OF WHAT JESUS DID FOR US ON THE CROSS.

BIBLE BASIS:
1 Corinthians 15:3–7,
51–58

MEMORY VERSE:
Christ has indeed been
raised from the dead,
the firstfruits of those
who have fallen asleep.
1 Corinthians 15:20

BIBLE BACKGROUND

Jesus' resurrection was a real historical event. Not only was His tomb empty (Luke 24:2–3, 12; John 20:3–8), but also there were witnesses! First Corinthians 15:3–7 lists numerous people who saw Jesus alive after His crucifixion, including more than 500 people at once. The Bible records at least 12 appearances of a risen Christ. The many firsthand accounts of the risen Lord offer additional credibility to the event. Although belief in Jesus still requires faith, the many who saw Him resurrected and reported it provides assurance of the event. Jesus' resurrection fulfilled what was foretold in Scripture.

Jesus defeated death. That's the great news of His resurrection. As a result, those who believe in Jesus as their Savior also will defeat death one day, through Christ, and live eternally.

No one has satisfactorily explained what could have happened to Jesus' body if He didn't rise from the dead. There were rumors that Jesus' disciples stole the body, but they died for their faith. Why would anyone die for a hoax? The Romans didn't steal the body because if they had, they would have brought it back out again when the Christians became so outspoken about their beliefs. Similarly, if the women had gone to the wrong tomb, the Romans would have revealed the correct tomb and shown people Jesus' crucified body. Some believed Jesus never actually died, but no one could survive a crucifixion and a burial. Jesus also was proclaimed dead, which is why the soldiers didn't break His legs, a customary way to speed up death during crucifixion.

Christ's victory over death was sin's final defeat. By dying on the cross and forgiving our sins, Jesus removed the punishment we deserved. By rising from the dead, Jesus gave us the victory over sin.

HINTS FROM THE KITCHEN

- This lesson encourages students to reflect on what Easter means. Jesus' resurrection wasn't just for Him; it impacts every Christian who believes in Him. We can share in eternal life because of Christ's work on the cross and His resurrection.

- As your students encounter non-believers they may find many people who agree that Jesus was a good person, but who draw the line at believing in someone who rose from the dead. After all, that seems to contradict what they know to be true about death. Death, they believe, is permanent. Counter such arguments by sharing that death can be tragic and sad, but for those who believe in Jesus it's not permanent. Begin by sharing that truth. After all, who wouldn't want to know more about how they can live forever in heaven? Jesus' resurrection is a great witnessing tool!

INGREDIENTS & SUPPLIES
(SERVES 10)

- ❑ 1 bag long, thick pretzel rods (at least 4 per student)
- ❑ 1 bag thin, red licorice rope
- ❑ Quick-hardening chocolate sauce
- ❑ Colorful candy sprinkles
- ❑ Wax paper
- ❑ Paper plates
- ❑ Resealable plastic bags

CREATIVE COOKERY

ALLERGY WARNING: There could be students who are allergic to chocolate or the wheat found in pretzels and licorice rope. If so, talk to them ahead of time to find out how they would like to make their crosses.

Use these promise crosses to remind you about Jesus' death and resurrection. If possible, make an extra cross to give to someone who doesn't know Jesus. What a great way to share what you believe!

1. Put colorful sprinkles on a paper plate.

2. Form a cross from two long pretzel rods.

3. Bind the cross together by wrapping one piece of thin, red licorice rope tightly around the center where the pretzels meet. Tie the ends of licorice together to hold it tight. (You may not need all of the licorice rope. Some licorice may require you to unravel larger licorice pieces to make a rope.)

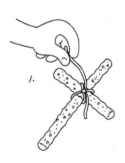

4. Squeeze some quick-hardening chocolate sauce onto a paper plate. Immediately dip the pretzel ends in the chocolate sauce.

5. Roll the chocolate-covered pretzel ends in sprinkles before the chocolate dries.

6. Set on wax paper until dry. Make as many crosses as you have pretzels. Enjoy!

7. Store remaining crosses in a resealable plastic bag.

SAVOR IT!

Jesus rose from the dead. It's a fact that gives all Christians great hope for a future life in heaven. Jesus rose; we share the victory!

> **What does Jesus' resurrection mean for you?** *(Answers may vary, but some might be that as a Christian, I can believe that I will be resurrected from the dead one day and will be in heaven with Jesus; Jesus conquered sin and death.)*

> **What are some ways you can share the victory of Jesus' resurrection with others?** *(share the reasons we know Jesus is alive, bring friends to church, encourage others to read the story of Jesus' death and resurrection, etc.)*

> **What are some of the evidences found in Scripture for Jesus' resurrection?** *(According to Matthew 28, Mark 16, Luke 24, and John 20—21, Mary, Peter, and John all saw the empty tomb; the twelve disciples and numerous other followers saw Jesus' resurrected body. First Corinthians 15:3–6 also reports that Jesus appeared to over 500 people at one time after his death.)*

PROMISE CROSSES

RECIPE TO TAKE HOME

Use these promise crosses to remind you about Jesus' death and resurrection. If possible, make an extra cross to give to someone who doesn't know Jesus. What a great way to share what you believe!

Ingredients:
- ❑ 2 long, thick pretzel rods (2 pretzel rods per cross)
- ❑ Thin, red licorice rope
- ❑ Quick-hardening chocolate sauce
- ❑ Colorful candy sprinkles

Supplies:
- ❑ Wax paper
- ❑ Paper plates

Directions:
1. Form a cross from two long pretzel rods.
2. Use one piece of thin, red licorice rope to tie the cross pieces together by wrapping it tightly around the center. Tie the licorice ends together to hold everything tight. (You may not need all of the licorice rope. Some licorice is sold in a package where you will need to unravel the larger pieces to make a rope.)
3. Squeeze some of the quick-hardening chocolate sauce onto a paper plate. Immediately dip the pretzel ends in the chocolate sauce.
4. Sprinkle colorful sprinkles over the chocolate-covered pretzel ends before the chocolate dries.
5. Set on wax paper until dry. Make as many crosses as you have pretzels.
6. Eat, then store remaining crosses in a resealable plastic bag.

GIFT GIVERS

THESE NO-BAKE COOKIE BALLS MAKE A GREAT GIFT.

BIBLE BASIS:
2 Corinthians 8:1–12

MEMORY VERSE:
For if the willingness is there, the gift is acceptable according to what one has, not according to what he does not have.
2 Corinthians 8:12

BIBLE BACKGROUND

Paul encouraged believers to help meet other believers' needs. There were many reasons Paul wanted the Corinthians, and all brothers and sisters in Christ, to demonstrate the grace of giving. In 2 Corinthians 8:8, Paul notes that giving is an evidence of the reality of love. In verse 7, Paul equates graceful giving with excellence in faith, speech, knowledge, earnestness, and love. In verse 9 Paul mentions that Jesus gave up His riches in heaven for believers. Paul also mentions that giving helps to meet others' needs (2 Cor. 8:14).

More important, however, than the gift is the attitude of the giver (2 Cor. 8:12). The saying, "It is better to give than to receive" rings true in this passage. The people in Macedonia were poor, yet they gave generously. They gave as much as they could and it was entirely their own idea to give. In 2 Corinthians 8:5 it says, "They gave themselves first to the Lord." What would it mean for us to give ourselves to God first and foremost? Wouldn't our possessions have less meaning to us if we truly did this?

If we compare ourselves with how most of the world lives, we're truly rich. We might not have the latest gadgets and may have a wish list of items, but sometimes these are actually things we can live without. Instead of saving up for yet another item that will be obsolete in a year, consider investing that money in God's kingdom. What you have to give can have a global impact if you will let it. We have much to offer others . . . so why hold back?

HINTS FROM THE KITCHEN

🍽 The thin chocolate or vanilla wafers should be crushed, but not too fine.

🍽 Making these balls will be messy so have wet paper towels on hand. Students can wipe their hands between rolling the balls and dredging them through the wheat germ.

🍽 Encourage students to thoroughly wash their hands before and after they have finished making the recipe.

INGREDIENTS & SUPPLIES
(SERVES 5)

- ❏ 1 package thin chocolate or vanilla wafer cookies (about 48 cookies)
- ❏ ½ cup caramel ice cream topping
- ❏ ¼ cup mini chocolate chips
- ❏ Wheat germ
- ❏ Large bowl
- ❏ Paper plates
- ❏ Large spoon
- ❏ Wet paper towels
- ❏ Optional: resealable plastic bags

CREATIVE COOKERY

ALLERGY WARNING: Be aware that some students might be allergic to the chocolate or the wheat in the cookies and wheat germ.

Simple cookies to make and share! Mix a batch up anywhere.

1. Prior to class, lightly crush (not too fine) all the wafers and place in a large bowl.

2. Have student volunteers mix wafers, caramel syrup, and mini chocolate chips together until the wafers and chocolate chips are covered and sticky.

3. Using clean hands, have students roll ingredients into one-inch balls that they place on a clean paper plate.

4. Have students clean their hands with a wet paper towel or wash hands if water is nearby.

5. Spread wheat germ on a different paper plate, then roll balls through the wheat germ until each ball is covered.

6. Have all students who participated in making them thoroughly wash their hands.

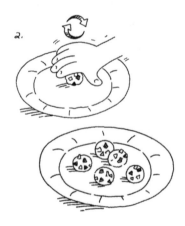

7. Enjoy these cookie balls in class or take home in resealable plastic bags.

SAVOR IT!

Money is one of those things . . . there never seems to be enough of it, yet God provides when you give it away according to His will. It might not seem to make sense, but for some reason that's how God often works with money. In fact, those who give generously their entire lives often can attest that God blesses them abundantly in return. Money isn't the only thing we can give, either. We can give our time, talent, and help and watch God use those gifts as well. Besides, giving to others is one of the greatest joys of the Christian life. When times are tough, those are the situations when you need to give more, not less. Although this concept may be hard to understand at first, the more you give the more you will want to give.

- Why do you think it's important to give with the right attitude? (*God looks at the heart. If the giving is not a reflection of what is in the heart, God really is not interested in the money amount; attitude is what counts.*)

- Money isn't the only way to help fill peoples' needs. How else can you give? (*You can give your time and abilities.*)

- What are some specific ways you can give? (*Give students time to answer.*)

NO BAKE CARAMEL CHOCOLATE CHIP BALLS

Simple cookies to make and share! Mix a batch up anywhere.

Ingredients:
- ❑ 1 package thin chocolate or vanilla wafers (about 24 cookies)
- ❑ ½ cup caramel ice cream topping
- ❑ ¼ cup mini chocolate chips
- ❑ Wheat germ

Supplies:
- ❑ Large bowl
- ❑ Paper plates
- ❑ Large spoon
- ❑ Wet paper towel (or sink for washing hands)
- ❑ Resealable plastic bags

Directions:
1. Lightly crush (not too fine) all the wafers and put in a large bowl.
2. Mix wafers, caramel syrup, and mini chocolate chips together until covered and sticky.
3. Using clean hands, roll ingredients into one-inch balls that you put on a clean paper plate.
4. Wash hands or use a wet paper towel to clean hands.
5. Spread wheat germ on a paper plate until the bottom of it is covered. Roll balls through the wheat germ.
6. Eat some and store some in a resealable plastic bag in the refrigerator to share with others!

Design & Devour
SCRIPTURE AND TOPIC INDEX

The following index allows you to use this book with any curriculum.
Simply find the Scripture your lesson is based on or the topic you are teaching.

Scripture	Topic	Page
Genesis 1:1–26	Creation	6
Genesis 1:28–31	Sin, the fall, salvation	10
Genesis 2:8–9	Sin, the fall, salvation	10
Genesis 2:15–17	Sin, the fall, salvation	10
Genesis 3:1–19	Sin, forgiveness	14
Genesis 6:9–10	God's faithfulness, the Flood	18
Genesis 7:1–5	God's faithfulness, the flood, obedience	18
Genesis 8:18–22	God's faithfulness, the flood, obedience	18
Genesis 12:1–7	Obedience	22
Genesis 15:1–6	Faith	26
Genesis 26:1–6	Perseverance	30
Genesis 26:12–25	Perseverance	30
Genesis 27:1–24	Family, honoring others	34
Genesis 27:30	Family, honoring others	34
Genesis 27:41	Family, honoring others	34
Genesis 33:1–11	Family, forgiveness	38
Genesis 49:29—50:21	God's control, sovereignty	42
Exodus 19:1–8	Ten Commandments	46
Exodus 19:20	Ten Commandments	46
Exodus 20:1–3	Ten Commandments	46
Matthew 1:18–21	Jesus' birth, Jesus is God's son	50
Matthew 3:13–17	Baptism	54
Matthew 6:9–13	Prayer, the Lord's Prayer	58
Mark 5:1–20	Mercy, power	62
Mark 11:12–14	Prayer	66
Mark 11:20–24	Prayer	66
Luke 5:1–11	God's power	70
Luke 7:18–23	Belief, doubt	74
John 1:1–18	Jesus was both God and man	78
John 1:35–45	Sharing Christ	82
John 3:1–8	Nicodemus, salvation	86
John 3:16–21	Nicodemus, salvation	86
John 3:36	Nicodemus, salvation	86
John 5:39–46	Salvation, belief	90
John 14:15–21	Holy Spirit	94
John 14:26	Holy Spirit	94
Romans 4:1–5	Faith	26
Romans 4:22–25	Faith	26
Romans 5:12	Sin, forgiveness	14
Romans 5:19	Sin, forgiveness	14
1 Corinthians 13	Love	98
1 Corinthians 15:3–7	Jesus' death and resurrection	102
1 Corinthians 15:51–58	Jesus' death and resurrection	102
2 Corinthians 8:1–12	Giving	106

Design & Devour
CORRELATION CHART
Each activity correlates to a Unit and Lesson in the curriculum lines shown below.
For further help on how to use the chart see page 5.

Title	Page	Scripture Reference	David C Cook BIL LifeLINKS to God College Press Reformation Press Wesley Anglican	Echoes The Cross
Uniquely Created!	6	Genesis 1:1–26	Unit 1, Lesson 1	Unit 1, Lesson 1
Following God's Trail	10	Genesis1:28–31; 2:8–9, 15–17	Unit 1, Lesson 3	Unit 1, Lesson 3
Saved from Our Dirt	14	Genesis 3:1–19; Romans 5:12, 19	Unit 2, Lesson 5	Unit 2, Lesson 5
Rainbow Twists	18	Genesis 6:9–10; 7:1–5; 8:18–22	Unit 2, Lesson 7	Unit 2, Lesson 7
A Buen Apetito Appetizer	22	Genesis 12:1–7	Unit 3, Lesson 9	Unit 3, Lesson 9
Stained-glass Crosses	26	Genesis 15:1–6; Romans 4:1–5, 22–25	Unit 3, Lesson 11	Unit 3, Lesson 11
Perseverance Ice Cream	30	Genesis 26:1–6, 12–25	Unit 3, Lesson 13	Unit 3, Lesson 13
Friendship Bread	34	Genesis 27:1–24, 30, 41	Unit 9, Lesson 9	Unit 9, Lesson 9
Fruit Pizza	38	Genesis 33:1–11	Unit 9, Lesson 11	Unit 9, Lesson 11
Colorful Kabobs	42	Genesis 49:29—50:21	Unit 9, Lesson 13	Unit 9, Lesson 13
Great Guides	46	Exodus 19:1–8, 20; 20:1–3	Unit 12, Lesson 10	Unit 12, Lesson 10
Angelic Substance	50	Matthew 1:18–21	Unit 4, Lesson 2	Unit 4, Lesson 2
Refreshingly Blue	54	Matthew 3:13–17	Unit 5, Lesson 6	Unit 5, Lesson 6
Prayer Chain	58	Matthew 6:9–13	Unit 11, Lesson 6	Unit 11, Lesson 6
Fiery Salsa	62	Mark 5:1–20	Unit 6, Lesson 12	Unit 6, Lesson 12
Fig-like Faith	66	Mark 11:12–14, 20–24	Unit 11, Lesson 8	Unit 11, Lesson 8
Power Bar	70	Luke 5:1–11	Unit 6, Lesson 10	Unit 6, Lesson 10
Honey Butter	74	Luke 7:18–23	Unit 7, Lesson 1	Unit 7, Lesson 1
Personified Parfaits	78	John 1:1–18	Unit 4, Lesson 4	Unit 4, Lesson 3
Eye-poppin' Dip	82	John 1:35–45	Unit 5, Lesson 8	Unit 5, Lesson 8
Frozen Cookie Delights	86	John 3:1–8, 16–21, 36	Unit 7, Lesson 3	Unit 8, Lesson 3
Salad Shakers	90	John 5:39–46	Unit 12, Lesson 12	Unit 12, Lesson 12
Healthy Boost	94	John 14:15–21, 26	Unit 8, Lesson 7	Unit 8, Lesson 7
Heartfelt Love Dip	98	1 Corinthians 13	Unit 10, Lesson 2	Unit 10, Lesson 2
Promise Crosses	102	1 Corinthians 15:3–7, 51–58	Unit 8, Lesson 5	Unit 8, Lesson 5
Gift Givers	106	2 Corinthians 8:1–12	Unit 10, Lesson 4	Unit 10, Lesson 4

ALLERGY ALERT LETTER TO PARENTS

DEAR PARENTS,

During the next year we will be doing fun *Design & Devour* creative foods in some class times. Please fill out the form below so the teacher will have it on file if your student has food allergies. Thank you for your help in ensuring that all our students are safe while they have fun crafting fabulous food that ties in with our Bible lessons.

In His Name,

Children's Ministry Coordinator

⬥

INFORMATION ABOUT STUDENT

Name: _____ Age: _____

Allergies: _____

Child reacts to ingesting allergens (typically) in this way: _____

_____

_____

Being touched by/exposed to an allergen (not just ingesting) can also cause the following allergic reaction:

_____

_____

_____

CONTACT INFORMATION

Father's (male guardian's) name: _____ Mother's (female guardian's) name: _____

Parents' or guardians' home phone number: (_____) _____

Parents' or guardians' pager, cell phone, or other way of contacting: (_____) _____

Treatment if exposed: _____

Number—in order—which to contact first:

☐ Parent or guardian (numbers listed above) ☐ Doctor's number: (_____) _____

☐ Hospital: (_____) _____ ☐ Allergist's number: (_____) _____

☐ 911

☐ Use EpiPen—Instructions (where stored, how to administer, etc.): _____

Parents can fill out this sheet with the help and input of their allergist, and append any needed information.

Signature : _____ Date: _____